Front-End Reactive Architectures

Explore the Future of the Front-End using Reactive JavaScript Frameworks and Libraries

Luca Mezzalira

Apress®

Front-End Reactive Architectures

Luca Mezzalira
London, Surrey, United Kingdom

ISBN-13 (pbk): 978-1-4842-3179-1
https://doi.org/10.1007/978-1-4842-3180-7

ISBN-13 (electronic): 978-1-4842-3180-7

Library of Congress Control Number: 2017964608

Managing Director: Welmoed Spahr
Editorial Director: Todd Green
Acquisitions Editor: Louise Corrigan
Development Editor: James Markham
Technical Reviewers: Antonio DeLuca and Massimo Nardone
Coordinating Editor: Nancy Chen
Copy Editor: Karen Jameson
Compositor: SPi Global
Indexer: SPi Global
Artist: SPi Global

Distributed to the book trade worldwide by Springer Science+Business Media New York, 233 Spring Street, 6th Floor, New York, NY 10013. Phone 1-800-SPRINGER, fax (201) 348-4505, e-mail orders-ny@springer-sbm.com, or visit www.springeronline.com. Apress Media, LLC is a California LLC and the sole member (owner) is Springer Science + Business Media Finance Inc (SSBM Finance Inc). SSBM Finance Inc is a **Delaware** corporation.

For information on translations, please e-mail rights@apress.com, or visit http://www.apress.com/rights-permissions.

Apress titles may be purchased in bulk for academic, corporate, or promotional use. eBook versions and licenses are also available for most titles. For more information, reference our Print and eBook Bulk Sales web page at http://www.apress.com/bulk-sales.

Any source code or other supplementary material referenced by the author in this book is available to readers on GitHub via the book's product page, located at www.apress.com/9781484231791. For more detailed information, please visit http://www.apress.com/source-code.

Printed on acid-free paper

To my Dad.

Table of Contents

About the Author

Luca Mezzalira is a System Architect with 15 years of experience, a Google Developer Expert on Web Technologies, and the London Javascript community Manager (`www.londonjs.uk`).

He had the opportunity to work on cutting-edge projects for mobile, desktop, web, TVs, set-top boxes, and embedded devices.

He is also an international speaker on Tech conferences with over 100 talks made in less than 10 years.

Luca thinks the best way to use any programming language is mastering their models; that's why he spends a lot of time researching topics such as OOP, Functional and Reactive programming.

With these skills, Luca can easily apply the best practices learned and drive any team to success.

He is also a natural leader, delivery focused, a problem solver, and a game changer; his passion is the driver for any activity, and he's able to make the difference in many circumstances.

In his spare time, Luca writes for national and international technical magazines and editors, and he's a technical reviewer for Apress, Manning Publications, Packt Publishing, Pragmatic Bookshelf, and O'Reilly.

About the Technical Reviewers

Antonio DeLuca is a fanatic of minimalist software development, accurate database design, and meticulous business analysis. He is focused on functional/object paradigms and service orientation. He has worked in various contexts and levels developing applications for the Web as well as other purposes with JavaScript/PHP, Java/C#, and other programming languages. He is based in London and is the Principal Software Developer at DAZN (a division of Perform Group).

Massimo Nardone has more than 23 years of experiences in Security, Web/Mobile development, Cloud, and IT Architecture. His true IT passions are Security and Android.

He has been programming and teaching how to program with Android, Perl, PHP, Java, VB, Python, C/C++, and MySQL for more than 20 years.

He holds a Master of Science degree in Computing Science from the University of Salerno, Italy.

Massimo has worked as a Project Manager, Software Engineer, Research Engineer, Chief Security Architect, Information Security Manager, PCI/SCADA Auditor, and Senior Lead IT Security/Cloud/SCADA Architect for many years.

Technical skills include the following Security, Android, Cloud, Java, MySQL, Drupal, Cobol, Perl, Web and Mobile development, MongoDB, D3, Joomla, Couchbase, C/C++, WebGL, Python, Pro Rails, Django CMS, Jekyll, Scratch, etc.

He worked as visiting lecturer and supervisor for exercises at the Networking Laboratory of the Helsinki University of Technology (Aalto University). He holds four international patents (PKI, SIP, SAML, and Proxy areas).

Currently he currently works as Chief Information Security Office (CISO) for Cargotec Oyj and he is a member of the ISACA Finland chapter board.

Massimo has reviewed more than 40 IT books for different publishing companies and is the coauthor of *Pro Android Games* (Apress, 2015).

Acknowledgments

I'd like to thank so many people that probably they wouldn't fit in just a page!

I think the most important one to mention though is my girlfriend Maela that is always here for me and she is the key to our family happiness.

Sometimes inspirations come in strange ways. I once read the story of the UFC champion Conor McGregor: he is really an interesting guy, sometimes with an overwhelming personality, but I think it is part of the role or mask he decided to wear.

McGregor made me think when I read this sentence:

"There's no talent here, this is hard work. This is an obsession. Talent does not exist, we are all equal as human beings. You could be anyone if you put in the time. You will reach the top, and that is that. I am not talented, I am obsessed."

To be honest, I totally agree. Everyone can be who he or she wants to be; it's hard and often we can be nearly there for giving up a dream, but our obsessions could really make the difference from failing to succeeding.

Several years ago, I would have never thought I'd be able to write an entire book in English and succeeding as a Software Architect outside my country – apparently my obsessions won.

CHAPTER 1

What Is Reactive Programming?

A journey of a thousand miles begins with a single step.

—Lao Tzu, *Tao Te Chang*

Have you ever heard about *Reactive Programming* or *Reactive Systems*? Do you think *React.js is a reactive library*? Have you ever thought about why you should use *Rx.JS inside an Angular project*? Is *Rx.JS* the new L*oadash*?

If at least one of these questions is often in your mind, this is exactly the right book to find an answer!

In these pages you will have a chance to learn more about reactive programming and reactive architecture for front-end development: a programming paradigm that is becoming more popular, every day, in the front-end community; but these days it is probably one of the most misunderstood and abused paradigm.

The main goal of this book is to provide a good understanding of what reactive programming is, how to use it in our projects, and particularly how to create fully reactive architectures for creating resilient and maintainable projects.

During this journey you will learn the following:

- What Reactive Programming is and why it's important

- What are the best use cases of this programming paradigm

- How to structure a fully Reactive architecture with different frameworks

- What will be the future of Reactive Programming on the front-end ecosystem

© Luca Mezzalira 2018

L. Mezzalira, *Front-End Reactive Architectures*, https://doi.org/10.1007/978-1-4842-3180-7_1

1

If you are wondering if the concepts learned inside this book are applicable also on a back-end architecture, my answer would be *YES, or at least, the majority of them could be applied to your back-end architecture too.*

Bear in mind that this book will focus the attention on front-end architectures with JavaScript, but some of the concepts illustrated should be easily portable to other back-end programming languages such as Node.js, for instance.

This book assumes that you already have good understanding of *JavaScript*, in particular *ECMAScript 6 and 7* syntax; *object-oriented programming;* and possibly some knowledge of *functional programming,* but it's not mandatory. Let the journey begin!

What Is Reactive Programming?

Every day when we open an editor or IDE to develop a program, we use our favorite programming language; sometimes we study a new one, but, consciously or unconsciously, we are making the decision of what kind of programming paradigm we are going to work with.

Reactive programming is not a new paradigm: it's one of the buzzwords we are used to hearing about in the JavaScript community in the past year or so, and it will become more than just a buzzword in the future.

I don't want to begin immediately by using too many technical terms because we will have enough time to learn about them while reading this book, but it's important that you understand what is the benefit of working in a "*reactive way.*"

If you read blog posts or articles on the Web, few of them are going to explain reactive programming with the spreadsheet cells example, where spreadsheet **cells are reacting to changes happening in other cells after user input**. This is definitely a good example but we can do better than this.

I'm sure you are familiar with the *dependency injection pattern* where an object is injected via the constructor or in a public method exposed by a class or module. This pattern leverages several benefits like decoupling between two objects and the possibility of testing the hosting object in isolation without creating dependencies and so on.

In some programming languages when we use dependency injection we are going to define an interface as function's argument in the hosting object and then we can interact with the methods available in the injected object.

The injected object in this case is used as an *interactive object,* because the host knows exactly what the contract is and how to use it.

In reactive programming instead, the hosting object will just subscribe to the injected one, and it will react to the propagation of changes during the application lifetime. See Figure 1-1.

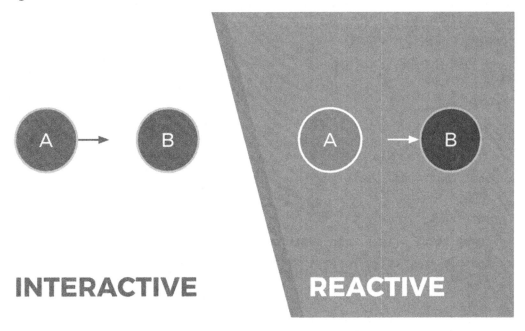

Figure 1-1. *Interactive vs. Reactive programming: in Reactive Programming the producer is A and the consumer is B*

Looking at the image above, we can immediately grasp the main difference between the two approaches:

- In the interactive example, object A is aware of which methods to call because knows exactly the B's object contract, also if we have to understand who has affected the state of the ingested object, we will search across all the projects that we are interacting with.

- In the reactive one, the contract is standard and object A is reacting to changes happened in object B, on top we are certain that any manipulation would occur inside the injected object; therefore we will have a stronger **separation of concerns** between objects.

- Because the hosting object is reacting to any value propagated inside the object injected, our program will be up to date without the need for implementing any additional logic.

It's time for a simple example before we move ahead with other concepts.

Let's assume we have a class called Calculator with a method sum and a class Receipt with a method print as shown in Listing 1-1.

Listing 1-1. Check Snippet1.js

```js
class Calculator {
  sum(a, b){
    return a + b;
  }
}

class Receipt {
  constructor(calculator){
    this.calc = calculator;
  }
  print(itemA, itemB){
    const total = this.calc.sum(itemA, itemB);
    console.log(`total receipt £${total}`);
  }
}

const pizza = 6.00;
const beer = 5.00;

const calc = new Calculator();
const receipt = new Receipt(calc);

receipt.print(pizza, beer);
```

As you can imagine, the program outputs *"total receipt £11."*

What we are doing in this example is creating the Calculator object and a Receipt object, and then we inject the Calculator instance called calc and we call the method print from the receipt instance with few arguments.

Inside the print method we are writing in the console the total price of the elements passed.

Checking the Receipt class implementation, you can spot in the print method that we are interacting with the method sum of the Calculator class and then getting the final result.

Now let's try to implement the same example in a reactive way in Listing 1-2.

Listing 1-2. Check Snippet2.js

```js
class Calculator {
  constructor(itemA, itemB){
    const obs = Rx.Observable.of(itemA, itemB);
    const sum$ = obs.reduce((acc, item) => (acc + item));

    return {
      observable: sum$
    }
  }
}

class Receipt {
  constructor(observable$){
    observable$.subscribe(value => console.log(`total receipt: £${value}`))
  }

}


const pizza = 6.00;
const beer = 5.00;

const calc = new Calculator(pizza, beer);
const receipt = new Receipt(calc.observable);
```

As you can see in this example, the Receipt class is subscribing to an object called observable, injected via the constructor, and all the logic of how to sum the prices and propagate them is delegated to the Calculator class. Therefore, the Receipt class is just reacting to a change, happening in a certain moment of the program's lifetime, displaying in the console the value emitted by the Calculator instance.

Another thing to highlight here is the contract between the objects: *instead of knowing exactly what method we should call, we pass an, with a default contract, and we react when something changes inside it.*

Overall, it's a very simple example but I hope it helps you to understand the shift of mindset we are going to have when we work with reactive programming; in the next few chapters we will see more reactive examples like this one.

Programming Paradigms

It's time to spend some words on programming paradigms to shed some light on reactive concepts and comparing them with functional and imperative programming.

Imperative Programming

Imperative programming is probably one of the most well-known programming paradigms.

Often, it's the first paradigm that we learn for understanding how a computer elaborates a program: it gives us all the tools for defining implementation details in depth and specifying exactly how a program should behave step by step.

Let's see an example of imperative programming:

```
class Calculator {
  constructor(){
    this.VAT = 22;
  }
  sum(...items){
    let total = 0;
    let i = 0;
    for(i; i < items.length; i++){
      total = total + items[i];
      total = total + items[i] * this.VAT/100;
    }
    return total;
  }
}

class Receipt {
  constructor(calculator){
    this.calc = calculator;
  }
  print(...items){
    let total = this.calc.sum(...items);
    console.log(`total receipt £${total.toFixed(2)}`);
  }
}
```

```
const JEANS = 80.00;
const SHIRT = 35.00;
const SHOES = 90.00;
const COAT = 140.00;
const HAT = 29.00;

const calc = new Calculator();
const receipt = new Receipt(calc);

receipt.print(JEANS, SHIRT, SHOES, COAT, HAT); //"total receipt £456.28"
```

Similar to the example discussed before, the sum method of the calculator object is accepting multiple arguments instead of just a couple, and we are summing all of them and applying the VAT value calculated per item.

As you can see, we are describing the exact implementation we want to perform: from defining a for statement in order to iterate trough the values in the array until expressing the VAT calculation for each single item.

Basically what we are doing is focusing on any implementation detail; potentially we could change the way we were iterating through the array's elements and start from the last element in the array instead of the first one or use a different variable name from "i"; these are the levels of detail we usually handle with imperative programming.

Now it's time to see how this example would be handled in functional and reactive programming.

Functional Programming

Functional programming is getting more famous on a daily base. Many languages arise embracing this paradigm and many existing languages are embracing it too for the readability, maintainability, and testability improvements.

If you are asking yourself why Functional Programming is becoming so popular, the answer can be found behind the concepts of this paradigm.

When we talk about Functional Programming we are talking about functions: in particular we are talking about **pure functions**.

A pure function is a function that, given an argument, is always returning the same result; it's predictable, easy to test, and doesn't generate any side effect inside the program.

Another important topic related to functional programming is the concept of **immutability**.

Immutability means that a specific value won't ever change during its life cycle, but if we need to manipulate it, we will create a new instance that contains the manipulated version of the original object.

Even if you are not familiar with this concept or have never dealt with it, I want you to see at least one concrete example.

Usually when you are dealing with an array and you want to iterate trough the values and interact with them in an imperative programming way, you would write something like this:

```
const originalArray = [1, 4, 8, 12];

for(let i = 0; i < originalArray.length; i++){
  originalArray[i] = originalArray[i] + 1;
}

console.log(originalArray) //[2, 5, 9, 13]
```

At this stage we have completely lost the initial values of the array called originalArray; if we want to have a copy of the initial values, we would create a new array that contains the modified values and then we would check that one.

In functional programming, instead, we are working by default with immutable objects; therefore, every modification we need to apply won't affect the original value but will generate a new one.

Taking into consideration the previous example, we could write in a functional programming way like this:

```
const originalArray = [1, 4, 8, 12];
const finalArray = originalArray.map(value => value+1);
console.log(finalArray); //[2, 5, 9, 13]
```

As you can see from these simple examples, functional programming is focused on what you are trying to achieve more than its implementation details.

That's a fundamental distinction compared to imperative programming. In fact, with functional programming we are describing our program, focusing on each action; and we need to do describe the data flow of our program more than focusing on each single detail such as which variable we have to define for iterating an array or how to increment the variable inside the for statement.

Another important aspect of software programming is how to deal with state management.

In Object-Oriented Programming we are used to encapsulating a state inside an object and changing it via different methods described in the same object. But in functional programming we are trying to compose it via pure functions that accept as the argument a state and return a new state.

Redux (http://redux.js.org/), a very well-known library in the React community, aims to resolve the problem of state management by implementing a state machine pattern.

In Redux, when we want to change the application state, we will need to call a method that accepts two arguments: the previous application state and an action. And it is returning the new state without mutating the previous one.

An Action is a simple object used for identifying in which state the application should transform.

Relying to pure functions will make our code more modular and more reusable, will create less bugs, and will suddenly become more testable!

Let's try now to convert the previous imperative example, porting it to functional programming. See Listing 1-3.

Listing 1-3. Check Snippet3.js

```
class Calculator {
  getTotal(...items){
    const total = items.map(::this.addVAT)
                      .reduce(this.sumElements);
    return total;
  }
  addVAT(itemValue){
    return itemValue + this.calculateVAT(itemValue);
  }
  calculateVAT(value){
    const VAT = 22;
    return value * VAT/100;
  }
  sumElements(accumulator, value){
    return accumulator + value
  }
}
```

```
class Receipt {
  print(total){
    console.log(`total receipt £${total.toFixed(2)}`);
  }
}

const JEANS = 80.00;
const SHIRT = 35.00;
const SHOES = 90.00;
const COAT = 140.00;
const HAT = 29.00;

const calc = new Calculator();
const receipt = new Receipt();

receipt.print(calc.getTotal(JEANS, SHIRT, SHOES, COAT, HAT)); // "total
receipt £456.28"
```

As we can see in the sum method implementation, we are focusing more on the actions we want to implement more than how to apply them; therefore, first we know that we need to calculate the VAT value for each single element (map method) and then to sum the items for retrieving the total (reduce method).

In this implementation we don't need to specify how we are iterating through the array elements or specifying variables to keep the state of the iteration; we just focus on our goal.

Another thing to notice in this implementation is how we are using functions as an argument of other functions; this mechanism is called **high-order functions** and it is another cornerstone of Functional Programming.

Obviously, Functional Programming is not just that: it is a broad topic with many other patterns to take in consideration like currying, practical application, memoization, and so on, but this is not the main topic of the book.

Bear in mind these concepts and possibly read a few posts online regarding them for mastering the different implementations because being familiar with Functional Programing will allow you to embrace Reactive Programming more easily.

If you are not used to thinking functionally, I strongly suggest peaking at a book that describes this paradigm in your favorite language; it's a great time investment, and you won't regret it.

Reactive Programming

We have just briefly seen Imperative and Functional Programming, but then what about Reactive Programming?

Reactive Programming is not a new concept – it's been a while since it has been used on server-side programming – but it's becoming very popular on the front-end ecosystem also.

We have seen how to easily turn a quick example to Reactive Programming, but it's not just that.

With Reactive Programming we could easily transform our code to Imperative Reactive Programming or Functional Reactive Programming.

The main concept behind this paradigm is the data flow and how an object observes and reacts to changes that happened during the life cycle of an application.

Let's start defining what Reactive Programming means:

Reactive Programming is a paradigm based on asynchronous data streams that propagate changes during the application life cycle.

What does it mean in practice? Let's assume we have to develop a financial dashboard, and all the data are coming from a server that is aggregating them for client visualization.

For the client we need to establish a polling mechanism or open a WebSocket communication for retrieving these pieces of information, and then we need to translate them into a nice user interface that will be consumed by our users.

Trying to decompose the challenge we want to implement and how we would be reasoning without Reactive Programming, consider the following:

1. We need to create a proxy, an action, or a command to retrieve the data from the server every few seconds, triggering the polling mechanism.

2. After retrieving the data, we need to analyze these data, possibly modifying or analyzing them to provide a friendlier visualization.

3. Then we pass these data to different components via a mediator, store, controller, or any other layer that is coupled with a view for updating it.

4. In the last part, we would be updating the DOM from the view, maybe highlighting only the data that have been changed since the previous change (in this case, a Virtual DOM mechanism could come to rescue minimising the effort).

There a quite a few parts to take care and lots of events, commands, or signals to use in order to make these data flowing from different parts of our application to display them in our views.

What would you say if you knew there is a better way to do it? It's a paradigm that will allow us to write less code and become more expressive and pluggable inside our current applications.

Obviously, I'm not saying we won't implement all these tasks – Reactive Programming is not a silver bullet or a magic wand – but we will learn soon that this paradigm could have quite a few surprises in store regarding its simplicity and expressiveness.

Another important concept on Reactive Programming is the way we are communicating within objects.

If you remember, a few paragraphs before, I showed an example of how we could solve a simple problem of communication between objects by injecting an observable instance instead of an instance of a specific class or module.

This could lead to many interesting scenarios that are currently not fully explored in the front-end panorama.

What would you say if the contract between objects become a standard one, and the instance we inject will have a predefined contract that will allow the hosting object to subscribe to changes from the injected instance?

This is not a new concept either: a similar idea was created in 1978 with Communicating Sequential Processes (CSP).

Despite the name, CSP allows you to work with sequential and parallel processes; a process is not more than a "channel" used for the asynchronous communication between objects.

In this way you are decoupling the objects using a channel for the communication; this channel though will allow you to not only pass data through it but to also do the following:

- aggregating data

- transforming data

- reducing data

- decorating data

On top of that, we will be able to manipulate channels (splitting, piping, merging, and so on) for creating sophisticated interactions between objects (Figure 1-2).

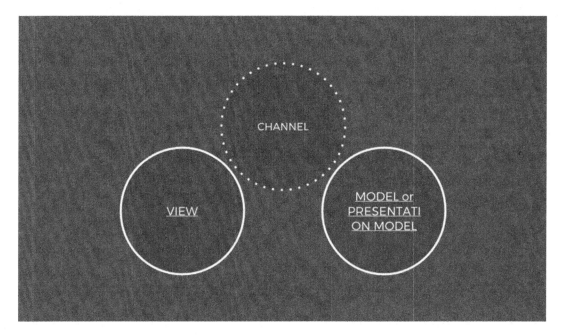

Figure 1-2. *In this diagram we are injecting a channel to the view and the controller, presentation model, mediator, or model for allowing the update of the view when the main state changes*

CSP is a fine-grained implementation of what we are going to explore in the Reactive world. If you are interested in spending some time with CSP, I'd suggest checking the library called CSP-JS (`https://github.com/ubolonton/js-csp`).

Understanding how CSP works will speed up your learning process on Reactive Programming.

After this brief digression we can move back to the main topic of this book; it's time now to see Reactive Programming in action in association with Imperative and Functional Programming.

Let's start with the Imperative example shown in Listing 1-4.

Listing 1-4. Check Snippet4.js

```
class Calculator {
  constructor(){
    this.VAT = 22;
  }
  sum(items){
```

```
        const items$ = Rx.Observable.from(items);
        const total$ = items$.map(value => value + (value * this.VAT/100))
                                    .reduce((acc, value) => acc + value);
    return total$;
  }
}

class Receipt {
  constructor(calculator){
    this.calc = calculator;
  }
  print(...items){
    const total$ = this.calc.sum(items);
    total$.subscribe(total => console.log(`total receipt £${total.
    toFixed(2)}`));
  }
}

const JEANS = 80.00;
const SHIRT = 35.00;
const SHOES = 90.00;
const COAT = 140.00;
const HAT = 29.00;

const calc = new Calculator();
const receipt = new Receipt(calc);

receipt.print(JEANS, SHIRT, SHOES, COAT, HAT);
```

In this example, we didn't change much compared to the imperative one, but let's analyze what we have done:

- In the print method of the Receipt object, we have transformed the arguments to an observable.

- We inject the observable to the sum method in the calculator class.

- There we are first applying the VAT to each single element via the map method.

- Then we sum these values and return another observable object.

- Last but not least, we subscribe to the observable object returned by the sum method, and we show the total price inside the console.

At this stage, I don't want to go in too much depth with reactive terminology; but for now think about an observable as an object that is wrapping the data and exposes some methods for manipulating the values – a sort of channel where data are flowing inside and we can apply transformation to these data.

After understanding how to implement some reactivity to Imperative Programming, let's see how the Functional example would look like, as shown in Listing 1-5.

Listing 1-5. Check Snippet5.js

```
class Calculator {
  getTotal(...items){
    const items$ = Rx.Observable.from(items);
    const total$ = items$.map(::this.addVAT)
                    .reduce(this.sumElements);
    return total$;
  }

  addVAT(itemValue){
    return itemValue + this.calculateVAT(itemValue);
  }

  calculateVAT(value){
    const VAT = 22;
    return value * VAT/100;
  }

  sumElements(accumulator, value){
    return accumulator + value
  }
}
```

```
class Receipt {
  print(total$){
    total$.subscribe(total => console.log(`total receipt £${total.
    toFixed(2)}`));
  }
}

const JEANS = 80.00;
const SHIRT = 35.00;
const SHOES = 90.00;
const COAT = 140.00;
const HAT = 29.00;

const calc = new Calculator();
const receipt = new Receipt();

receipt.print(calc.getTotal(JEANS, SHIRT, SHOES, COAT, HAT));
```

Also in this case, the example is pretty much the same but now the Receipt is using the observable called total$ that got a different signature from the previous example where we got just a simple number.

Once again, an observable allows subscribing to it and retrieving the values that are flowing inside it.

At first glance these concepts could seem unimportant, but they will help us a lot when we try to create a full reactive architecture.

When Should You Use Reactive Programming?

Often, when a new trend is rising, a lot of developers are used to abusing the new technology or framework (hype-driven development). As we understood during this chapter, Reactive Programming is used for handling the propagation of data during the life cycle of an application. Therefore, a perfect fit for this paradigm would be a real-time data application like a financial dashboard or any monitoring system for instance. In a nutshell, we can say that any application that is heavily data driven could be a great fit for Reactive Programming.

Obviously, it doesn't mean you shouldn't use this paradigm in other applications, but real-time web apps and applications with a large amount of asynchronous transactions and mutations are where Reactive Programming really shines.

If we decide to use Reactive Programming inside existing architectures, such as Angular or Redux, for instance, it could be a good design decision because it could facilitate the update of our views or the state propagation inside components.

Nowadays the Web is full of plenty of reactive examples, libraries and frameworks are raising them with great success, and embracing them will impose a shift of mindset in order to embrace the real power of this paradigm.

Another great benefit of Reactive Programming is the simplicity of testing your code and describing data flows in a concise but clear manner.

Reactive Programming is already implemented in production environments of several large organizations such as Netflix, Google, and Microsoft.

Microsoft and Google, for instance, are a great contributor of the Reactive Programming movement (`http://reactivex.io/`).

Netflix, as well, is another company that is contributing heavily to the evolution of this paradigm with Rx.JS 5, and Reactive Programming is applied in several implementations currently in production.

How Should You Write an Application Fully Reactive?

One night I went to a meetup in London where we were discussing the JavaScript trends for 2017. Funny enough, Reactive Programming was one of these trends and the facilitator asked a question to all of the attendees: "How many of you are working with Reactive Programming now?" And half of the room raised their hands asserting a positive answer. After this question, the facilitator asked the following one: "How many of you are using React.js only as Reactive library?" Then over 85% of the people that raised their hand at the previous question raised their hand again.

That wasn't surprising for me because it provides an understanding how few people are interpreting Reactive Programming in a correct way.

We could decide to structure our projects with a fully Reactive architecture where the communication/interaction between objects, the state management, and the interaction with endpoints are all handled in a Reactive paradigm.

Reactive Programming on the front end and back end brought up different architectures and implementations that are interesting to use but at the same time different from what we are used to dealing with.

In this book we are going to explore different approaches currently available inside the front-end Reactive community.

CHAPTER 2

Architectures Comparison

If you think good architecture is expensive, try bad architecture.

—Brian Foote

In this chapter we are going to explore the current status of front-end architectures. When we pick a framework for our projects, someone else made decisions for us on how to structure an architecture following best practices and design patterns for giving us the freedom to make design decisions, focusing mainly on what our applications should achieve more than how to structure them.

It's important here to highlight the difference between architecture and design because often these terms are misunderstood.

When we talk about architectures, we are defining how our system is going to interact between different elements. For example, think about the communication between a model and a view. Usually when we define architecture we are defining the relationship between objects, how they communicate between each other, and so on. Architectural decisions are hard to change because they usually drive a project in a specific direction, which would require a huge effort for moving it in a different direction.

Design decisions, instead, are local decisions like choosing a specific library, algorithm, or design pattern for solving a problem in our project.

When we make a design decision on a project, it often doesn't require a huge effort recovering from it, but in certain situations making poor design decisions will lead to a long refactoring of our system. Let's assume we need to solve a problem where every few minutes we need to refresh the data inside a specific view without refreshing the entire page but only the elements that need to change; we could decide to use React.js for its diff algorithm or create our own algorithm where we could have more control defining a diff algorithm close to our needs.

19

© Luca Mezzalira 2018
L. Mezzalira, *Front-End Reactive Architectures*, https://doi.org/10.1007/978-1-4842-3180-7_2

Sorting out the difference between architecture and design decisions, it's time to see what we are going to explore in this chapter.

The front-end ecosystem is in continuous evolution, in particular in the past few years where we were experiencing different but fundamental changes that are improving the creation and maintainability of our projects.

We are probably living the most exciting decade of the past 10 years, overwhelmed by revolutionizing concepts that are often coming from the past but with a new twist, transforming them in useful ways and taking actual approaches for solving our daily challenges.

The front-end architectures changed a lot in the past 30 years, as we moved from the classic Model View Control (MVC) to more actual architectures that nowadays are present in many contemporary frameworks.

This could be a representation in a timeline of this evolution. During this chapter we are going to see in action the most famous architecture and we are going to compare them.

Figure 2-1 shows a timeline where I highlighted all the architectures and implementations we are going to explore and in what year they were created. You will see that many concepts from the 1980s or '90s are very contemporary and used in the most famous framework implementations currently available in the JavaScript ecosystem.

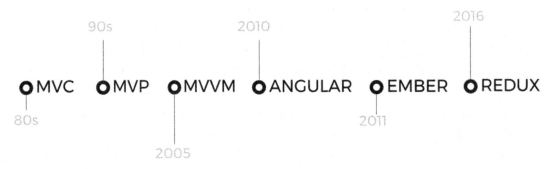

Figure 2-1. *Architectures timeline*

The most important thing to remember is that these architectures are not obsoletes but that they are still valid concepts to use, and they can add a lot of value to our projects by drastically facilitating the development and maintenance of them. Creating well-structured and flexible architectures also provide us the agility needed to embrace not only design changes but architectural ones as well.

Also, we need to bear in mind that these architectures can be converted to Reactive architectures if we apply the Reactive concepts in a proper way; therefore if our project is currently using one of them, we can still embrace the Reactive model, applying a few changes to enhance them and moving to a more reactive paradigm.

MV* Architectures

In this section, we are going to dig into the base concepts of MV* architectures; in order to do that we will work on a simple project (a basic calculator) for understanding how these architectures are composed, and how objects are communicating by embracing the SOLID principles that any project should take in consideration in order to be maintainable and extensible.

The three architectures we are going to explore in this section are MVC, MVP, and MVVM; let's start with the oldest one, MVC!

S.O.L.I.D.   SOLID is a set of principles created by Uncle Bob. SOLID is an acronym that stands for:

S – Single-responsibility principle

O – Open-closed principle

L – Loskop substitution principle

I – Interface segregation principle

D – Dependency inversion principle

If you are interested in knowing more about them, I suggest watching this Uncle Bob lecture: **https://www.youtube.com/watch?v=t86v3N4OshQ**

Bear in mind though, that all the code presented in this chapter are just highlights of the final examples; therefore if you have a hard time following the snippets, feel free to download the chapter examples first and switch from this book to your favorite editor or IDE for consulting the code.

Remember first to install all the dependencies with the command:

```
npm install
```

And then you can run the n.p script called build in this way:

```
npm run build
```

Model View Control

Model View Control (MVC) is an architectural pattern introduced in Smalltalk in the late 1980s by Trivet Reenskaug, and it is probably the most popular architecture of the past 30 years, used by millions of developers in any project independently of the language used (Figure 2-2).

Its main characteristic is the separation of concerns and the single responsibility of its actors; the main innovation of this pattern was finally separating the data from their visual representation, a concept not fully explored until then.

In fact the model objects are completely separated from their representation; therefore there isn't any knowledge of the view inside the model.

This detail becomes important when multiple views or controllers are accessing the same data because our model objects could be reused across different screens without any problem.

MVC is based on three basic principles:

- *Model*: where the application state and domain data live

- *View*: the user interface of our applications interacted on by the users

- *Controller*: the glue between the model and the view, usually responsible for orchestrating the communication flow inside the application

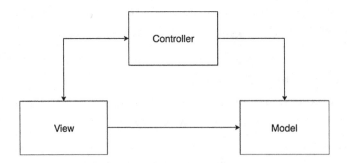

Figure 2-2. *Model View Control diagram (MVC)*

How MVC Works

Usually the controller instantiates the view and the model in the constructor or, in certain implementations, are injected by the main application class via dependency injection. The relation between a controller and the views could be one to many, so a controller could handle multiple views: the same relationship is valid for the models as well.

When we want to scale up this architecture for large projects usually we try to split up these relationships in order to have almost a 1 to 1 relation between these three objects so we can reuse components that are self-contained and architected in the same way the entire application works, like a Russian doll.

As described before the main aim of a model is storing the application state and everything that should be persistent across a single or multiple views, usually every time the application state changes or data are updated; the model is triggering an event in order to update the view.

In the vast majority of implementations the object listening for any state or data change is the view, but in certain implementations we can also find a total separation between the model and the view where the controller in this case is listening to the change and is propagating this information to the view.

The view is simply responsible for displaying the application data and listening for any user interactions.

Figure 2-3 shows how MVC works with an implementation of a calculator in JavaScript.

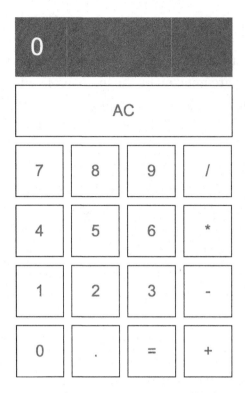

Figure 2-3. *This is the output of our Calculator application*

This is the final result of what we want to achieve.

It is a simple calculator where every time we are clicking a button, we add the value on the display on the top and when the user is going to click the button "=" we will display the result.

Let's start to explore our MVC example from the controller. See Listing 2-1.

Listing 2-1. CalculatorController.js

```
initialize(){
        const emitter = this.initEmitter();
        this.model = this.initModel(emitter);
        this.initView(emitter, this.model);
 }
```

In our implementation, the controller is going to instantiate the view and the model, and it's injecting an event emitter for communicating between objects via events. This will immediately improve the decoupling between objects because if in the future we want to reuse some of these objects in other projects, we won't need to copy more than the object we are interested in, considering they are communicating via events, and as long as we respect the contract our code becomes reusable and flexible.

We are going to use React.js for handling the views of our project.

React usually renders the components again when there is a properties update, but in our case what we implement is using the event bus for notifying the view that a new result should be rendered on the calculator's display, and then the view will retrieve the data from the model, updating with the new string the display.

In order to do that, we need to inject the model and the emitter instance inside the view. See Listing 2-2.

Listing 2-2. CalculatorController.js

```
initView(emitter, model){
        const cont = document.getElementById("app");
        ReactDOM.render(<Calculator emitter={emitter} model={model} />,
        cont);
}
```

Then we will use the React Component life-cycle methods to store these two objects locally and listen for any change from the model; when a change happens, we are going to update a state property inside the React component to display the correct value. See Listing 2-3.

Listing 2-3. Calculator.jsx

```
componentWillMount(){
        this.model = this.props.model;
        this.emitter = this.props.emitter;
        this.emitter.on("TotalChanged", _ => this.setState({displayValue:
        this.model.total}));
        this.setState({displayValue: this.model.total})
}
```

So, every time the displayValue property is updated, this will trigger the render function; therefore the view will be updated with a new result as shown in Listing 2-4.

Listing 2-4. Calculator.jsx

```
render(){
        return(
            <div>
                <div style={displayStyle}>{this.state.displayValue}</div>
                {this.createRow("row1", "AC")}
                {this.createRow("row2", "7", "8", "9", "/")}
                {this.createRow("row3", "4", "5", "6", "*")}
                {this.createRow("row4", "1", "2", "3", "-")}
                {this.createRow("row5", "0", ".", "=", "+")}
            </div>
        );
    }
```

Inside the model instead, we are going to keep the application state, handling what should be displayed in our view and performing some calculations.

Our model is composed by a few methods that will allow the controller to call every time a button is clicked from the Calculator keyboard as you can see in the following code in Listings 2-5 and 2-6.

Listing 2-5. CalculatorController.js

```
initEmitter(){
        let emitter = new LiteEventEmitter();
        emitter.on("CalculateEvent", _ => {
            this.model.calculate();
        });

        emitter.on("AddValueEvent", content => {
            this.model.addValue(content.value, content.type);
        });

        emitter.on("ResetEvent", _ => {
            this.model.reset();
        })

        return emitter;
    }
```

Listing 2-6. CalculatorModel.js

```
calculate(){
    this.totalOperation = math.eval(this.totalOperation);
    this.state = FIRST_OPERATION;
    this.emitter.emit("TotalChanged");
}

addValue(value, type){
    if(type === NUMERIC){
        this.totalOperation = this.getValue(value);
    } else if(type === SYMBOL){
        this.totalOperation = this.checkSymbol(value);
    }

    this.state = IN_PROGRESS_OPERATION;
    this.emitter.emit("TotalChanged");
}

reset(){
    this.totalOperation = 0;
    this.state = FIRST_OPERATION;
    this.emitter.emit("TotalChanged");
}
```

The Controller, via the emitter object, is listening for any event triggered by the view and it is requesting to the model to perform some operations like reset, calculate, or add a new value.

The model, instead, every time `totalOperation` value is changing it, notifies via the event bus our view that will display the new value updating the state property of our React component, triggering then the render function.

MVC is a pretty simple and straightforward pattern: there is a good separation of concern, each object has a unique responsibility, and all the information is well encapsulated.

Model View Presenter

Model View Presenter (MVP) is an architecture created in the 1990s, and one of its first appearances was made in IBM software (Figure 2-4). From my point of view, MVP shines when we need to reuse views or behaviors in different projects or different areas of the same application; with this architecture we start to give more importance to the modularization of our front-end applications and provide architecture specific for a front end more than a generic one that could fit a back-end or front-end application like for MVC.

MVP is very helpful, in particular, when we work on cross-platform applications and we want to reuse the application data, communication layer, and behaviors or when we want to swap the views changing them at runtime or compile/transpile time.

The main differences between MVP and MVC could be summarized in the following list:

- Having a presenter instead of a controller, we will see in a moment which benefits come in with a presenter.

- The relation between a view and a presenter is not 1 to many like in MVC but is always 1 to 1.

- The best MVP implementation for having reusable components is when we design our views as passive views because swapping them becomes easier as long the contract between the presenter and the view is respected.

Figure 2-4. *MVP diagram where the view is unaware of the model's existence*

How MVP Works

The presenter object is inspired by the presentation model pattern, and my favorite implementation is when the presenter is designed as a Supervising Controller where it retrieves all the data useful for a view from the model, and at the same time it should handle any user interaction updating the model. As mentioned before, the views are passive or if you prefer dumb, they just know how the rendering logic works, possible animations, integration with CSS styles, and so on.

On top, the presenter is also dealing with updating the model and retrieving the information needed for rendering a view. Usually, in complex applications, you could have a persistent model (or more than one model maybe exposed by a façade) across the entire life cycle of an application and multiple presenters that retrieve and update the application data in the models.

Another important point to highlight is the fact that the model and the view should not be aware of each other; maintaining these two completely isolated from each other will help a lot in the case of large applications or when we need to swap views for targeting different devices.

Imagine for a moment that our assignment is a project where we need to target different devices like browsers, mobile, and smartTVs – exactly the same application but different UI for different targets considering that each target has different input methods and UI patterns.

With an MVP architecture, maintaining the behaviors inside the presenter, the business domain in the model and having just passive views for the UI will allow us to have similar behaviors across the application, reusing the same code for the models and changing the views – adapting them for the device we are targeting without much effort.

Passive View   A passive view is a view without any knowledge of how the system works but just relying on another object for handling the communication with the system. A Passive view doesn't even update itself by retrieving data from the model; this view is completely passive, and its main scope is focusing on what to render on the screen when a specific render function is called from a controller or presenter.

Supervising Controller   A supervising controller is a specific type of controller that is handling user interaction as well as manipulating the view for updating it. When a supervising controller is present in an architecture, the view needs only to redirect the user events to the supervising controller (in MVP the presenter is our supervising controller), and it will take care of handling the logic and updating the view with new data.

The supervising controller is responsible for the communication in the system and it's taking care to update the view it is associated with.

It's time to see MVP in action with the Calculator example discussed above, but this time with the Model-View-Presenter in mind.

We can start from the App.js file where in the constructor we are going to create the model and the presenter, and we import the view called Calculator.jsx.

We then inject React component and model inside the presenter as shown in Listing 2-7.

Listing 2-7. App.js

```
export default class App{
    constructor(){
        const mainModel = new CalculatorModel();
        const mainPresenter = new CalculatorPresenter();
        mainPresenter.init(mainModel, Calculator);
    }
}
```

Then we can move inside the presenter where we are going to store all the objects injected in variables and then we render the React component injected. See Listing 2-8.

Listing 2-8. CalculatorPresenter.js

```
initialize(model, view){
        this.model = model;
        this.view = view;
        this.cont = document.getElementById("app");
        this.renderView();
}
renderView(){
        const component = React.createElement(this.view, {result: this.
        model.total, onBtnClicked: ::this.onBtnClicked});
        ReactDOM.render(component, this.cont)
}
```

In our Presentation model we are injecting the model and the view for having complete controls on them; we then call the method renderView that will be our trigger for communicating to a React component to render again because something happened inside the application and the UI should be updated.

As you can see, the view doesn't have any knowledge of the model but we pass the result to display in our calculator via the props object exposed by React.

Now it's time to take a look at the view; and as we defined at the beginning of this section, the view should be a passive view, so in this case it is taking care of what to render and how nothing else should be integrated in a passive view.

The communication with the presenter is happening via a method passed via the props object. Like we have seen in the renderView method, the presenter is passing a callback that should be invoked every time the user is selecting a button of our calculator. See Listing 2-9.

Listing 2-9. Calculator.jsx

```jsx
import React from "react";
import ReactDOM from "react-dom";
import {ulStyle, acStyle, btnStyle, displayStyle} from "./Calculator.css";

export default class Calculator extends React.Component{
    constructor(props){
        super(props);
    }

    componentWillMount(){
        this.btnClicked = this.props.onBtnClicked;
    }

    onButtonClicked(evt){
        evt.preventDefault();
        this.btnClicked(evt.target.innerHTML);
    }

    createRow(id, ...labels){
        const items = labels.map((value, index) => {
            return <li key={`${id}_${index}`}
                    style={value === "AC"? acStyle : btnStyle}
                    onClick={::this.onButtonClicked}>
                {value}
            </li>;
        })
```

```
        return(
            <ul key={id} style={ulStyle}>
                {items}
            </ul>
        )
    }

    render(){
        return(
            <div>
                <div style={displayStyle}>{this.props.result}</div>
                {this.createRow("row1", "AC")}
                {this.createRow("row2", "7", "8", "9", "/")}
                {this.createRow("row3", "4", "5", "6", "*")}
                {this.createRow("row4", "1", "2", "3", "-")}
                {this.createRow("row5", "0", ".", "=", "+")}
            </div>
        );
    }
}
```

All the methods present in the React component are defined for rendering the correct button or the display, and this.props.onBtnClicked is the method passed by the presenter.

This method is identifying which button was selected so the presenter can capture the user interaction and it calls the correct method exposed inside the main model as you can see in the snippet below in Listing 2-10.

Listing 2-10. CalculatorPresenter.js

```
onBtnClicked(value){
        switch (value) {
            case "AC":
                this.model.reset();
                break;
```

```
        case "=":
            this.model.calculate(value);
            break;
        case "+":
        case "-":
        case "/":
        case "*":
        case ".":
            this.model.addValue(value, SYMBOL);
            break;
        default:
            this.model.addValue(value, NUMERIC);
            break;
    }

    this.renderView();
}
```

It's time to see what the model is doing; in this case the model is taking care of all the calculations and maintaining the application state. That will facilitate the debugging of our application because we know that the view is dealing merely with the UI of our application, and the presenter is handling the user interactions and the model keeps the application state and the caching of application data.

Let's take a look to the model shown in Listing 2-11.

Listing 2-11. CalculatorModel.js

```
export default class CalculatorModel{
    constructor(){
        this.totalOperation = 0;
    }

    calculate(){
        this.totalOperation = math.eval(this.totalOperation);
        this.state = FIRST_OPERATION;
    }
```

```
    addValue(value, type){
        if(type === NUMERIC){
            this.totalOperation = this.getValue(value);
        } else if(type === SYMBOL){
            this.totalOperation = this.checkSymbol(value);
        }

        this.state = IN_PROGRESS_OPERATION;
    }

    checkSymbol(value){
        const str = this.totalOperation;

         if(this.state === FIRST_OPERATION){
            return str + value;
        }

        return !isNaN(str.charAt(str.length - 1)) ? str + value : str.
        substr(0, str.length - 1) + value
    }

    getValue(value){
        return (this.totalOperation == 0 || this.state === FIRST_OPERATION)
? value : this.totalOperation + value;
    }

    reset(){
        this.totalOperation = 0;
        this.state = FIRST_OPERATION;
    }

    get total(){
        return this.totalOperation;
    }
}
```

As you can see in the model, there are all the methods called by the presenter, like reset or calculate, and a few others like checkSymbol and getValue, used for handling the application logic.

The separation of concerns in MVP is very strong and any application would be easier to debug and maintain if we properly apply these few concepts; it's definitely an architecture that largely improved the MVC concept created 10 years before it.

Model View View-Model

Model View View-Model (MVVM) is an architecture created by Microsoft in 2005 for handling the GUI management with Windows Presentation Foundation (WPF). It sticks with a true separation between the view and the model like we have seen in the MVP architecture, but MVVM encapsulates few differences compared to other architecture (Figure 2-5).

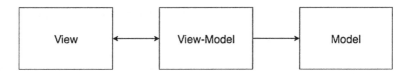

Figure 2-5. *MVVM diagram, similar to MVP but the view is not a passive one anymore*

How MVVM Works

The first difference is that we have a View-Model instead of a presenter; this specific object will be the bridge between the data stored inside a model and the view.

In a nutshell the view-model is responsible for exposing the data present inside the model to the view and it is also responsible for preparing the data in a way that the view expects, so you can immediately understand that the logic of the view-model is tightly coupled with what the view should render.

For instance, let's imagine that we have a stock value stored in the model with dollars currency but the view needs it to be shown in euro. In MVVM the model stores the raw data, that is, dollars value, and the view-model would be responsible for converting the value to a given currency, in this case euro.

Another important aspect of the View-Model is the fact that it has a relationship with the views that is 1 to many: therefore we can have one view-model that is handling multiple views or components.

The communication of the View-Model and the view usually happen via bindings; therefore every time a value is updated on the view or in the View-Model, this value is communicated to the other object in order to keep it in sync.

It's very important to understand that with MVP we enforced the concept of complete separation between the model and the view and in MVVM this strong concept doesn't change at all.

The model is very simplistic; we store data in a raw format without any particular change, and in this case we should even avoid keeping the state in the model and moving this information to the view-model or even the view if it's a small component.

Let's see now how our calculator would work with an MVVM architecture.

The App.js file is instantiating all the objects for an MVVM architecture: model, view-model, and view; in the view-model constructor we are going to inject the model and view instances so it will be able to retrieve data from the model and serve the view with the correct value to display. See Listing 2-12.

Listing 2-12. App.js

```
export default class App{
    constructor(){
        const model = new CalculatorModel();
        const emitter = new LiteEventEmitter();
        const vm = new CalculatorViewModel(model, emitter);

        const cont = document.getElementById("app");
        ReactDOM.render(<Calculator emitter={emitter}
        initValue={model.total} />, cont);
    }
}
```

The Calculator view is a React component that has two key concepts: dispatching the data from the view to the view-model and retrieving the data from the view-model.

In order to do that we can use a data binding library or simply events as both are accepted from MVVM architecture, therefore we are using an event emitter, injected when the view and the view-model were instantiated, for handling the communication between these two objects, as shown in Listing 2-13.

Listing 2-13. Calculator.jsx

```
componentWillMount(){
        this.setState({displayValue: this.props.initValue})
        this.emitter = this.props.emitter;
        this.emitter.on("UpdateDisplayValue", value => this.setState
        ({displayValue: value}));
    }
manageDisplayState(value){
        switch (value) {
            case "AC":
                this.emitter.emit("ResetEvent")
                break;
            case "=":
                this.emitter.emit("CalculateEvent")
                break;
            case "+":
            case "-":
            case "/":
            case "*":
            case ".":
                this.emitter.emit("AddValueEvent", {value: value,
                type: SYMBOL})
                break;
            default:
                this.emitter.emit("AddValueEvent", {value: value,
                type: NUMERIC})
                break;
        }
    }
```

In manageDisplayState we have all the events we will communicate to the view-model, but in the componentWillMount we define only the event we need to listen for updating the calculator's display.

The rest of the view is very similar to the other views we have discussed in the previous examples.

Now it's the turn of our view-model. Here we need to do exactly the opposite of how we handled the events in the view; therefore we are going to listen for all the events emitted by the view and dispatch the event for updating the view's display every time the value changes. See Listing 2-14.

Listing 2-14. CalculatorViewModel.js

```
initialize(){
        this.emitter.on("CalculateEvent", _ => {
            this.calculate()
        });

        this.emitter.on("AddValueEvent", content => {
            this.addValue(content.value, content.type);
        });

        this.emitter.on("ResetEvent", _ => {
            this.reset();
        })
}

updateDisplayAndState(state){
        this.state = state;
        this.emitter.emit("UpdateDisplayValue", this.model.total);
}
```

The view-model is responsible for retrieving and updating the data stored in the model, so every time the user clicks a button in our view we are going to update the value in the model and then call the `updateDisplayAndState` method for dispatching this change to the view.

We keep a state internal to the view-model to understand which method we need to call during the calculation; therefore we need to update it when the state is changed.

Let's see, for instance, how we handle the changes in the three methods we have created for handling these operations, as shown in Listing 2-15.

Listing 2-15. CalculatorViewModel.js

```
addValue(value, type){
        let valueToAdd;
        if(type === NUMERIC){
            valueToAdd = this.getValue(value);
        } else if(type === SYMBOL){
            valueToAdd = this.checkSymbol(value);
        }

        this.model.add(valueToAdd)
        this.updateDisplayAndState(IN_PROGRESS_OPERATION)
}

reset(){
        this.model.reset();
        this.updateDisplayAndState(FIRST_OPERATION)
}

calculate(value){
        this.model.calculate(value);
        this.updateDisplayAndState(FIRST_OPERATION)
}
```

All of them are doing two main operations:

1. They are updating the model.

2. They are dispatching to the view the new value to display.

It's now clear that the majority of application business logic is present in the view-model; therefore if we want to reuse a specific component or part of the application. we need to maintain the event or the binding contract between the view and the view-model as it is. So we can say that these two objects become slightly more tightly coupled compared to their relation in the MVP architecture.

Last but not least, it's time to discuss the model. As you can see, the model just exposes a few methods in order to update the value to display; it doesn't have any data manipulation or any state, and in this case the model is just a data representation of the main application so if we need to use it in combination with another view-model, the model will provide the data expected and nothing more. See Listing 2-16.

Listing 2-16. CalculatorModel.js

```
export default class CalculatorModel{
    constructor(){
        this.totalOperation = 0;
    }

    calculate(operation){
        this.totalOperation = math.eval(this.totalOperation);
    }

    add(value){
        this.totalOperation = value;
    }

    reset(){
        this.totalOperation = 0;
    }

    get total(){
        return this.totalOperation;
    }
}
```

JavaScript Frameworks

Now that we have explored the basics of MV* architectures, understanding the benefits and the issues related to each of them, it's time to review what the JavaScript ecosystem is proposing and how these architectures are implemented.

I'm sure you will realize very soon that understanding the three architectures mentioned before will help you to capture the technical approaches provided by well-known frameworks like Angular, Ember, or Redux.

In this section we are going to re-create our calculator application three more times: the first one with Angular, then with Ember, and we will conclude this journey with the combination of React and Redux.

Angular

Angular is an open source framework created and maintained by Google. It's been around since 2010 and has reached recently version 5, but from now on Google explained that we should just call it Angular.

This framework passed through different stages in the past years, from a huge hype when launched with version 1; then, after the announcement of version 2 not being retro compatible with the previous version, many developers decided to move away from it and embrace other frameworks – in particular, React and Flux or Redux or similar combinations.

Recently, as in 2017, Google released a new version that should enhance the experience of the JavaScript developers with Angular, providing a complete ecosystem of tools and patterns in order to work easily with this framework without the need to scrap the Web for assembling multiple libraries inside the same project.

Since version 2, Angular embraces TypeScript as its main language; JavaScript ES6 and Dart are supported too, but the vast majority of the resources in the Angular website are prepared with TypeScript.

Angular as a framework is providing a full architecture and utilities out of the box with also an interesting CLI tool for speeding up a developer's productivity.

TypeScript   TypeScript is a typed superset of JavaScript, and it enhances the language adding Enum, Generics, Abstract, and Interfaces very familiar with strictly typed languages like Java, for instance.

More information on the official website: **https://www.typescriptlang.org**

How Angular Works

The architecture we will evaluate in this section is related to Angular 2 and onward (Figure 2-6), so we won't take into consideration the previous one because it works in a different manner.

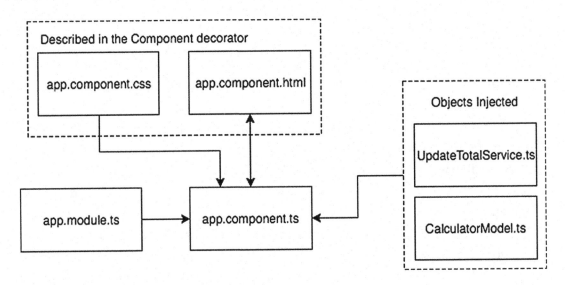

Figure 2-6. *Angular architecture example*

Angular architecture introduces four interesting concepts:

- Dependency Injection

- Modularity with NgModules and Components

- Data binding between Templates and the Components

- Large use of decorators for defining the objects like Components or Modules

We will now go more in depth of this architecture, analyzing the different parts that compose an Angular project.

Any Angular application has at least an NgModule called the root module; an NgModule is not like a normal JavaScript Module. The peculiarity of the NgModule is the metadata; in each NgModule (root module included), we will describe how the module is composed, and in particular we will define which components belong to a module, if a module has dependencies from other modules, directives, or components; and we also describe the services used by the components present in the module.

As described before, any Angular application contains at least one module called the root module.

For instance, this is the root module created for our Calculator project in Angular:

```
import { BrowserModule } from '@angular/platform-browser';
import { NgModule } from '@angular/core';

import { AppComponent } from './app.component';

@NgModule({
  declarations: [
    AppComponent
  ],
  imports: [
    BrowserModule
  ],
  providers: [],
  bootstrap: [AppComponent]
})
export class AppModule { }
```

As you can see in this code snippet, Angular is largely made up of decorators (@NgModule) for wrapping our code inside the Angular framework.

Decorators   The decorators in JavaScript are actually in proposal (stage 2) for becoming part of the language (more information on the proposal at this link: **https://github.com/tc39/proposal-decorators**).

They are based on a simple concept: a decorator wraps a function, augmenting its functionalities without manipulating the function decorated.

Usually, in a decorator, we add methods or properties that should be common in our project at runtime; that's why Angular is using a large number of them. It's so we can write our logic without inheriting from some base class, thereby creating a tight coupled connection between and decorating it with the built-in functionalities available in the framework.

The next topic to introduce is the Angular components. Since Angular 2 we have the possibility to create components, and we can think of them like a bridge between the template system present in Angular and the data we can retrieve from REST API or specific endpoints. Their role is mainly retrieving the data and populating the template with new data via a binding system that is present out of the box in Angular 2.

The Angular component is a mix of properties we can find in the presenter and the view-model. In fact, the following is true:

- A component is updating the view via binding like in the view-model object.

- The relation between a component and a template is always 1 to 1 like for the presenter.

- The component handles all the user interaction happening in the template like for the presenter.

In order to define a component in Angular we need to specify another decorator, @Component. For our calculator example, we have defined just one component considering how simple the application is; but potentially we could have split them in multiple parts as shown in Listing 2-17.

Listing 2-17. App.component.ts

```
const ON_SCREEN_KEYBOARD = [
  ['7', '8', '9', '/'],
  ['4', '5', '6', '*'],
  ['1', '2', '3', '-'],
  ['0', '.', '=', '+']
];

@Component({
  selector: 'app-root',
  templateUrl: './app.component.html',
  styleUrls: ['./app.component.css'],
  providers: [UpdateTotalService, CalculatorModel]
})
export class AppComponent implements OnInit {
  onScreenKeyboard = ON_SCREEN_KEYBOARD;
  total:string;
```

```
constructor(private updateTotalService:UpdateTotalService){}

ngOnInit(): void {
  this.total = this.updateTotalService.reset();
}

updateTotal(value: string){
  switch (value) {
    case 'AC':
        this.total = this.updateTotalService.reset();
        break;
    case '=':
        this.total = this.updateTotalService.calculate();
        break;
    case '+':
    case '-':
    case '/':
    case '*':
    case '.':
        this.total = this.updateTotalService.addSymbol(value);
        break;
    default:
        this.total = this.updateTotalService.addValue(value);
        break;
  }
 }
}
```

As you can see in the decorator (@Component) we are specifying the HTML template and the CSS associated with the component. The objects to inject will be accessible inside the component but they will be instantiated by Angular and a selector that is just an ID to identify the component.

The last thing to mention about Angular components is that we can use life-cycle hooks like ngOnInit method that is triggered when the component is initialized and in our case we use it to set the first value in our calculator display.

Now it's time to see how the components interact with templates. Angular has its own way to handle HTML markup; we can use some directives in order to iterate through a data structure for displaying multiple HTML elements or for adding specific attributes if a certain condition happens in our code.

Directives   Directives in Angular are instructions for the HTML template on how the template should handle the DOM.

In our example we have associated an `app.component.html` template to the `app.component.ts` described above and this is the code used for the template:

```
<div class="displayStyle">{{total}}</div>
<div class="acStyle" (click)="updateTotal('AC')">AC</div>

<ul *ngFor="let row of onScreenKeyboard">
    <li *ngFor="let value of row"
      class="btnStyle"
      (click)="updateTotal(value)">
      {{value}}
    </li>
  </ul>
```

In this code it is important to highlight a few concepts. The first concept is that the binding with the `total` property is created inside the component, so every time we are updating this value, the new value will automatically be displayed inside our template.

The other interesting thing is how we have created the buttons in our calculator; we are iterating an array present in the component object and with *ngFor directive we are creating multiple tags with different values; then, when a user clicks on the button we are calling the method updateTotal passing the button's label; also in this case we use Angular markup for triggering the user interaction (`(click)="updateTotal(value)"`).

Interestingly enough, just with few lines of code. Angular provides a simple but very powerful mechanism of data binding, templating, and styling our views.

It's time to talk about the dependency injection part; as we saw in the component decorator we are defining an array of providers. Basically we are injecting UpdateTotalService and CalculatorModel to the component.

The CalculatorModel won't be used by the component but if we want to inject this object inside the service, we need to specify it there.

What is a Service in Angular? A Service is inspired to the Command Pattern, and it's used for fetching data from an endpoint or for retrieving/passing data to a model like in our case.

Command Pattern   The command pattern is a behavioral pattern. A command contains all the objects needed to perform an action when a specific event happens inside an application such as user interaction, data fetching, and so on.

Usually the command pattern has an interface with just one public method called execute; and after instantiation, where we can inject the objects needed for performing the action, we can call this method for performing the logic described inside the command.

Usually the command is used for decoupling the interaction within objects like the controller and model or presenter and model, and then we maintain them totally decoupled.

This is our `UpdateTotalService` class as shown in Listing 2-18.

Listing 2-18. UpdateTotalService.ts

```
@Injectable()
export class UpdateTotalService{
    constructor(private model:CalculatorModel){}

    calculate(){
        this.model.calculate();
        return this.model.total;
    }

    addValue(value){
        this.model.add(value, VALUE);
        return this.model.total;
    }
```

```
addSymbol(value){
    this.model.add(value, SYMBOL);
    return this.model.total;
}

reset(){
    this.model.reset();
    return this.model.total;
}

}
```

This service exposes a few methods that will be used for manipulating the model in a specific way.

The model is injected in the constructor via the framework; therefore when we call this.updateTotalService.reset(); from the component class we won't need to have any knowledge of the model but the service will return the value retrieved from the model, isolating the view from the model like we have seen in the MVVM pattern, for instance.

Another important thing to notice in this class is the injectable decorator provided by Angular for describing a class that is injected inside a component; just adding this decorator, the framework knows when to instantiate and inject.

The last part to describe is our model that is a very basic model with some knowledge on how to manipulate the data to store. Here again we are using the @injectable decorator for the possibility of being injected by Angular. See Listing 2-19.

Listing 2-19. CalculatorModel.ts

```
@Injectable()
export class CalculatorModel{
    private state:string;
    private totalOperation:string;

    constructor(){
        this.state = FIRST_OPERATION;
        this.totalOperation = '0';
    }

    get total(){
        return this.totalOperation;
```

```
    }

    reset(){
        this.totalOperation = 'O';
        this.state = FIRST_OPERATION;
    }

    add(value, type){
        if(type === VALUE){
            this.totalOperation = this.getValue(value);
        } else {
            this.totalOperation = this.checkSymbol(value);
        }
        this.state = IN_PROGRESS_OPERATION;
    }

    calculate(){
        this.totalOperation = math.eval(this.totalOperation);
        this.state = FIRST_OPERATION;
    }

    checkSymbol(value){
        const str = this.totalOperation;

        if(this.state === FIRST_OPERATION){
            return str + value;
        }

        return !isNaN(Number(str.charAt(str.length - 1))) ? str + value :
        str.substr(0, str.length - 1) + value
    }

    getValue(value){
        return (this.totalOperation === 'O' || this.state === FIRST_
        OPERATION) ? value : this.totalOperation + value;
    }
}
```

Our model is a simple object that contains the source of truth for our application, maintaining the state and the value that should be displayed inside the views.

Just to summarize the Angular calculator example: we have seen the key concepts of Angular, we also noticed quite a few similarities with MVVM and MVP architectures like the relation between view and template or who is handling the user interactions. The last thing worth mentioning is that Angular can become a reactive architecture pretty easily, because it incorporates Rx.js library inside the framework; therefore, within a certain degree, we can twist this architecture to a Reactive one almost out of the box.

Ember

Ember is a framework oriented to web applications. It's well-known in the JavaScript community and used by large organizations such as Netflix or Groupon.

Ember has an interesting ecosystem composed by EmberCLI, EmberData, and Ember as a JavaScript framework.

The paradigm behind Ember is slightly different from other frameworks but the productivity is high if the application fits this paradigm.

Ember favors convention over configuration; a key thing to remember is embracing the EmberCLI tool because it will facilitate your life and boost your productivity, the CLI takes care to generate all the files needed for a specific view (template, router, unit testing files, and so on), model, route, or even controller.

The Ember framework shines when a project has an architecture "fat server – thin client" where the majority of the logic is handled on the server; the client should be as dumb as possible and it should be a multipage application over a single page application (SPA).

How Ember Works

Ember architecture (Figure 2-7) is based upon MVVM architecture, and there are some key elements that composed this framework:

- Routes
- Templates
- Components
- Controllers
- Models

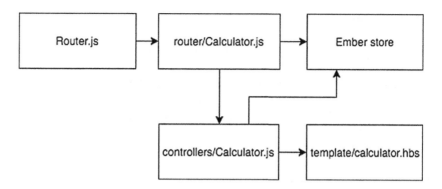

Figure 2-7. *Ember architecture example*

In Ember everything starts from a route module and each view is tightly coupled with the endpoint associated. By default any Ember application has a main route system where we define all the application routes; for instance, in our calculator application we have defined this route shown in Listing 2-20.

Listing 2-20. Router.js

```
Router.map(function() {
  this.route('calculator', {path: "/"});
});
```

That means the root of our web application will be routed to the calculator route. Because Ember works with conventions, we need to save the modules in the right folders in order to be picked up. But luckily the Ember CLI comes to the rescue by providing some useful commands that prepare all the files needed out of the box:

```
Ember generate route <name>
```

And automatically the CLI will generate a route file, the associated test file, and the template, and then it will also insert the code for the new route to the application route system.

The route we created for our calculator exposes the model to the template; in Ember only the routes and the controllers have access to the model. Therefore, there is a strong separation of concerns between the view and how the model should be in an MVVM architecture.

```
export default Ember.Route.extend({
    model(){
        this.store.push({
            data:[{
                id: 1,
                type: "calculator",
                attributes: {
                    total: "0",
                    state: AppState.FIRST_OPERATION
                },
                relationships: {}
            }]
        });

        return this.store.peekRecord('calculator', 1);
    }
});
```

The concept of Model in Ember is slightly different from what we are used to; the Model class defines that the value will be present in the store (the concrete model) facilitating the data validation when they hit the client side of our Ember application.

If we check our model class, present inside the models folder, we can see that we are defining two properties" both of type string, one called total and the other state. See Listing 2-21.

Listing 2-21. models/calculator.js

```
import DS from 'ember-data';

export default DS.Model.extend({
    total: DS.attr("string"),
    state: DS.attr("string")
});
```

As you can see from the route code above, the store is a data structure centralized for the entire application (think of it as a Singleton), accessible by the routes and controllers, so independently from the amount of templates, routers, or controllers our application is composed of, we have a unique source of truth to fetch or cache data.

The store object is a very interesting one because it allows data to be automated and fetched from an endpoint, and then it will store the response directly inside the store object without handling all the code for defining these kinds of operations.

The store works with records; a record is a concrete model that contains the data fetched from a REST endpoint or cached inside the application like in our case.

It's very important to notice the structure of an object stored in a record, as shown in Listing 2-22.

Listing 2-22. routes/calculator.js

```
{
     id: 1,
          type: "calculator",
          attributes: {
               total: "0",
               state: AppState.FIRST_OPERATION
          },
          relationships: {}
}
```

Inside the store we need to define the data object with a unique ID; a type value, used for retrieving it later on; and the attributes we need to store inside it, for our application will be the value total and the application state.

Because we are not fetching the data from any remote endpoint we are using peek Record method, which will skip the server request and retrieve the data directly from the concrete model.

Instead if we would need to retrieve data from a specific REST endpoint, we could use find Record that will perform a request to the endpoint specified, and it will store the response inside the store object.

Our application logic sits in the controller where we are providing public methods for the views to be called and we are handling the setting and getting of data to and from the model.

When we extend the base controller from the Ember framework we have an object called actions where we can expose all the methods to the template; in our case we just have one method called updateTotal:

```
export default Ember.Controller.extend({
    onScreenKeyboard: [
        ["7", "8", "9", "/"],
        ["4", "5", "6", "*"],
        ["1", "2", "3", "-"],
        ["0", ".", "=", "+"]
    ],
    actions:{
        updateTotal(value){
            let result;
            let model = this.store.peekRecord('calculator', 1);

            switch (value) {
                case "AC":
                    model.set("total", 0);
                    model.set("state", AppState.FIRST_OPERATION);
                    break;
                case "=":
                    result = math.eval(model.get("total"));
                    model.set("total", result);
                    model.set("state", AppState.FIRST_OPERATION);
                    break;
                case "+":
                case "-":
                case "/":
                case "*":
                case ".":
                    result = checkSymbol(model.get("total"), value, model.
                    get("state"));
                    model.set("total", result);
                    model.set("state", AppState.CALCULATING);
                    break;
```

```
        default:
            result = getValue(model.get("total"), value, model.
            get("state"));
            model.set("total", result);
            model.set("state", AppState.CALCULATING);
            break;
        }
    }
  }
});
```

Here in each case we are retrieving the current value from the store and manipulating it, but the annoying part is that Ember works a lot with strings in order to identify a specific object or value. Therefore we won't have code completion provided by our editor and it could be prone to error if it's not properly wrapped in a constant statement.

The last bit to discuss is the template. Ember is using handlebars out of the box; therefore if we are familiar with this famous template library we will be productive in no time.

Handlebars has some specific markup, like Angular, for identifying specific behaviors like filtering, creating similar tags populated with data retrieved from the controller or the route and so on.

This is the handlebars code needed in order to render our calculator:

```
<div class="displayStyle">{{model.total}}</div>
<div class="acStyle" {{action "updateTotal" 'AC' on="mouseDown"}}>AC</div>
{{#each onScreenKeyboard as |row|}}
<ul>
  {{#each row as |value|}}
    <li class="btnStyle" {{action "updateTotal" value
    on="mouseDown"}}>{{value}}</li>
  {{/each}}
</ul>
{{/each}}
```

It's interesting to highlight how we handle the method exposed by the controller via the action command:

```
{{action "updateTotal" value on="mouseDown"}}
```

We identify the method name passing a parameter called value in this case, and specifying when the method should be invoked: in this case on mouse down.

To summarize, Ember is a really productive framework based on MVVM architecture with a lot of common activities ready to be used out of the box. It favors convention over configuration, it has a reach ecosystem composed by different tools and libraries, and the documentation is really exhaustive.

React + Redux

React and Redux is a combination of libraries that together can resemble a minimal framework with a large ecosystem that is not imposed at the beginning like for Ember or Angular but is more oriented to a plug-in system where we can use what we really need without the need to import everything up front.

React is a library useful for manipulating the DOM, based on components as first citizen; it takes care of the view part of an architecture only, implementing smart algorithm like the reconciliation one – a diff algorithm used for rendering only the part of the DOM that should change.

React introduced a very powerful concept embraced nowadays by several other libraries: the Virtual DOM. The Virtual DOM is a DOM representation where the diffing algorithm operates at first glance and where React understands what should change and when, minimizing the changes to the real DOM and improving the performances of our web applications.

Reconciliation   Reconciliation is a key concept for React. If you want to know more, I suggest reading the official documentation regarding this topic: https://react-cn.github.io/react/docs/reconciliation.html

---

On the other hand, Redux is a state container not tightly coupled with React because we can find examples of Redux used in combination with other frameworks like Angular.

Redux is solving a well-known problem of how to manage the state inside an application.

The most interesting part of it is that it leverages a concept introduced in 2015 from another library called Flux, created by Facebook, of **unidirectional flow**.

Unidirectional flow is a powerful but simple concept: the objects communication inside an application should be unidirectional, and this, in combination with good encapsulation, will allow any application to be easier to debug, to be picked by any team because also complex applications are easy to understand and debug, thereby improving the code quality and the possibility of extending them.

The Redux paradigm is straightforward and is composed by only three key elements:

- Actions
- Reducers
- Stores

The action is just a plain JavaScript object containing the information of what happened inside the application.

The reducer is retrieving from an action that the interaction happened in the application and knows how the state should change based on the action dispatched.

Finally, the store is the object that brings all together; the store is passing to the reducer the current state tree and the action, and it waits until the reducer provides back the new state, then the store will append to the state tree and all the objects that are listening for a change will be notified.

Redux was created on top of three core concepts:

- Single source of truth: the application state is represented inside a tree defined inside a single object called store.

- State is read-only: the only way to change the state with Redux is via an action.

- Changes are made with pure functions only: the reducers are pure functions that are receiving the current state tree and an action, and they know how the application will change to the next state. If we always pass the same parameters, we know the output of a pure function; in this case the reducer will be always the same.

Let's see React and Redux in action with our calculator example written for the last time with a different architecture.

How Redux Works

The starting point of any Redux project (Figure 2-8) is usually a main application where we create the store object and we wrap our main view inside a provider object from the Redux library. See Listing 2-23.

Listing 2-23. App.js

```
export default class App{
    constructor(){
        const store = createStore(CalculatorReducer);
        const cont = document.getElementById("app");

        ReactDOM.render(
            <Provider store={store}>
                <CalculatorContainer/>
            </Provider>, cont);
    }
}

let app = new App();
```

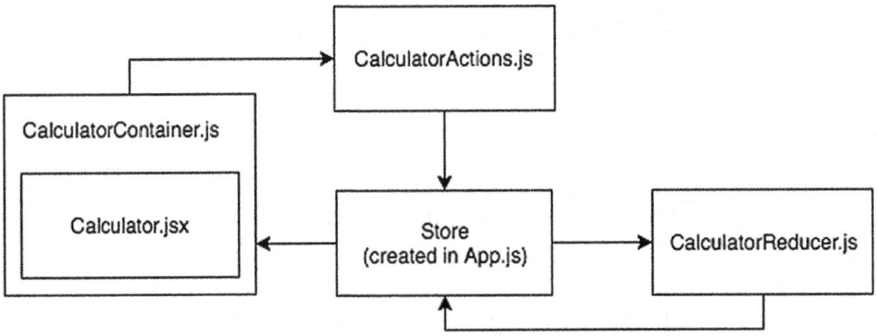

Figure 2-8. *Redux project architecture diagram*

As we mentioned before, after creating the store and associating it to a specific reducer (Calculator Reducer), we are wrapping our main view (Calculator Container) inside a **Provider object** from the redux library.

Think about the Provider as an object that receives as input the store and it propagates it to all the container components inside an application in order to have complete access to it.

Considering we have mentioned the container components, it's time to move to the view part, where we need to distinguish between presentational components and container components.

The creator of Redux, Dan Abramov, wrote a post on Medium.com regarding this topic where is explaining the difference between the two types of components.

To summarize Dan's thoughts, in Redux we distinguish the presentational components as component with the only scope of managing the look and feel of the view, more or less like the **Passive View** described in this chapter. Meanwhile we identify the container components as the ones that can handle the presentational component logic like user interactions, having access to the store, and mapping the store values to the React component via a props object, similar to the **Supervising controller** of the MVP architecture.

This approach will lead to a better separation of concern and reusability of our components across different projects.

Presentational vs. Containers components   In Redux this is a very important topic. I strongly suggest having a look at this link to Dan Abramov's Medium post on the **presentational and containers** components explanation: **http://bit.ly/1N83Oov**

Based on what we have just described, it's time to see what a presentational component looks like and how we handle the communication with the Redux framework.

In the calculator example, our presentational component code looks like that shown in Listing 2-24.

Listing 2-24. Calculator.jsx

```
export default class Calculator extends React.Component{
    constructor(props){
        super(props);
        this.onBtnClicked = this.props.onButtonClicked;
    }

    createRow(id, ...labels){
        let items = labels.map((value, index) => {
            return <li key={`${id}_${index}`}
```

```
                    style={value === "AC"? acStyle : btnStyle}
                    onClick={::this.onBtnClicked}>
                    {value}
                </li>;
        })

        return(
            <ul key={id} style={ulStyle}>
                {items}
            </ul>
        )
    }

    render(){
        return(
            <div>
                <div style={displayStyle}>{this.props.result}</div>
                {this.createRow("row1", "AC")}
                {this.createRow("row2", "7", "8", "9", "/")}
                {this.createRow("row3", "4", "5", "6", "*")}
                {this.createRow("row4", "1", "2", "3", "-")}
                {this.createRow("row5", "0", ".", "=", "+")}
            </div>
        );
    }
}
```

We can immediately spot that we are focusing more on what our component looks like than what it does. The only method that is going to be used is the onButtonClicked method retrieved from the props object as well as the result property that will be used to show the calculation inside the calculator display div element.

The entire logic of this component as well as the communication with the rest of the application is made inside the container component, as shown in Listing 2-25.

Listing 2-25. CalculatorContainer.js

```javascript
const mapDispatchToProps = (dispatch) => {
    return {
        onButtonClicked: (evt) => {
            evt.preventDefault();
            let value = evt.target.innerHTML
            manageDisplayState(value, dispatch);
        }
    }
}

const manageDisplayState = (value, dispatch) => {
    switch (value) {
        case "AC":
            dispatch(reset())
            break;
        case "=":
            dispatch(calculate())
            break;
        case "+":
        case "-":
        case "/":
        case "*":
        case ".":
            dispatch(appendValue(value));
            break;
        default:
            dispatch(appendValue(value));
            break;
    }
}
```

```
const mapStateToProps = (state) => {
    return{
        result: state.result
    }
}
```

```
export default connect(mapStateToProps, mapDispatchToProps)(Calculator);
```

In this module, we can find many interesting things like the following:

- The presentational component is created after calling the connect method. The connect method is used to "connect" the store to the component, and it returns a higher-order React component class that passes state and action into our component derived from the supplied arguments.

- mapStateToProps is the method we use in order to translate the new state passed by the store into properties that will be rendered in the presentational component.

- mapDispatchToProps is the method we use to trigger all the dispatch actions happening inside our container component. The dispatch method accepts an action that will be triggered and listed into the store and passed to the reducer.

Before we move to the reducer, it's good to understand what an action is. Basically an action is just a plain JavaScript object. Inspecting the CalculatorAction module, we can see it clearly in Listing 2-26.

Listing 2-26. CalculatorActions.js

```
export function calculate(){
    return {
        type: CALCULATE
    }
}
```

```
export function reset(){
    return {
        type: INIT,
        result: 0
    }
}

export function appendValue(value){
    return {
        type: APPEND,
        toAppend: value
    }
}
```

The actions are similar to commands where they bring with them the information needed to the reducers in order to change the current state to a new one. Usually they have a property type where we define the type of action called from the store.dispatch method.

Finally, it is the turn of the reducer. The reducers are used when we need to change the application state, because the action is notifying us that something happened inside the application but it doesn't have the knowledge of how the application should change – that's the reducer's duty. See Listing 2-27.

Listing 2-27. CalculatorReducer.js

```
const calculation = (state = reset(), action) => {
    switch (action.type) {
        case CALCULATE:
            return {
                type: action.type,
                result: math.eval(state.result)
            }
            break;

        case APPEND:
            return {
                type: action.type,
                result: resultHandler(state, action.toAppend)
            }
```

```
            break;
        case INIT:
            return {
                type: action.type,
                result: resultHandler(state, action.toAppend)
            }
            break;
        default:
            return state;
            break;
    }
}
```

In our reducer, we set as the default state the reset action that starts the application with the initial state (INIT in our switch statement).

Every time an action is dispatched, the store calls the reducer passing the current state and the action dispatched, and then the reducer is mapping the action to the next application state.

Redux is a very simple but effective state management library, and it's interesting that there are many similarities with the MVP architecture – in particular for the relation view presenter like we have in Redux with the presentational component and its container.

Also in the redux ecosystem there are other libraries that we can use in combination with Rx.js, for instance, or other reactive libraries.

Wrap-Up

In this chapter, we have evaluated different architectures from the oldest one like MVC to the most recent one like Redux. We saw a clear evolution of them but with many references to the past principles. Often we spend a lot of time with a framework without asking us why the authors picked one decision over another. I hope that this journey through the most famous architectures/frameworks available for the front-end development provided you some benefit in your future projects because I truly believe that it is very important to have a good knowledge of them for choosing the right one for a specific project. Too often I have seen developers and architects always using the same architecture fitting any project inside it instead of using "the right tool for the right job".

From the next chapter on, we are beginning the Reactive journey that will lead us to learn how reactive architectures work from different point of views and we will discover more about Cycle.js, MobX and SAM.

CHAPTER 3

Reactive Programming

All life is an experiment. The more experiments you make the better.

—Ralph Waldo Emerson

After an overview of the most famous front-end architectures and their implementations, it's time to dig into the main topic of this book: Reactive Programming with JavaScript.

I watched many videos and read many articles and books on the argument, and I have to admit that often I had the impression that something was missing, like we were just scratching the surface instead of going in depth inside the Reactive ecosystem.

The main aim of this chapter is to provide all the tools needed for understanding Reactive Programming more than focusing on a single library, embracing the concepts behind this programming paradigm. This should allow us to embrace any reactive library without the need to invest too much time for switching our mindset.

I often saw developers embracing a specific library or framework and being real ninjas with them, but once moved away, they struggled with approaching different implementations – mainly because they didn't understand what there was behind the implementation.

Understanding the core principles of the reactive paradigm will allow you to master any library or framework independently from the different implementations without treating just as a "black box."

There are many reactive libraries available in the open source ecosystem and, we are going to discuss the most famous like Rx.JS and XStream. After that we are going to understand the key principles of Reactive programming such as what is a stream, the difference between hot and cold observables, and back pressure.

Unfortunately, reactive programming has a high learning curve mainly due to the concepts it is leveraging, but once you get used to them, you will start reasoning in a reactive way for everything without any issue.

© Luca Mezzalira 2018
L. Mezzalira, *Front-End Reactive Architectures*, https://doi.org/10.1007/978-1-4842-3180-7_3

Reactive Programming 101

First and foremost, implementing reactive programming means working mainly with *events streams*, but in order to understand what an event stream is, we should start with a simple diagram for better understanding how a stream works.

Figure 3-1 is called a *marble diagram* and it is used to represent an event stream.

Figure 3-1. *Marble diagram representation example*

It's very important to understand how it works because often in the documentation you can understand how the APIs work by just looking at the diagram without the need to read the full explanation.

Also, marble diagrams are useful during the testing phase because when we need to simulate an event stream, we will use them against our event stream implementation. But let's see what they are so we can understand better the concept of event stream.

In a marble diagram, we can spot a horizontal line representing the time (our stream), and the value inside the colorful circles are events that are happening at a certain point in time in our application (events).

The vertical line, instead, represents the end of our stream, after that point the stream is completed.

So if we want to describe this diagram we can easily do it in this way:

- After the application started, a stream emits the value 4.

- After a certain amount of time, the stream emits the value 1 and right after 3.

- After all these events, the stream was completed.

The stream could also end after an error, and in that case instead of seeing a vertical line, the marble diagram (Figure 3-2) will show an **X symbol** notifying when the error happened inside the stream.

Figure 3-2. *Marble diagram with error*

The last bit to mention is when we apply transformation to the values inside a stream via operators.

An operator is a method that allows us to manipulate the data in a stream or the stream itself.

In this case the marble diagrams can show how the values are transformed like in this example with the *map operator* where we are adding 1 to any number emitted by the stream on the top and creating a second stream with the values manipulated (Figure 3-3).

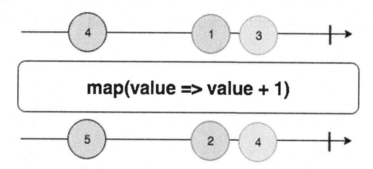

Figure 3-3. *Marble diagram with map operator applied to an initial stream that returns a new stream with data manipulated*

Until now, we understood that an event stream is a sequence of values (events) passed in a certain period (stream).

We can then assume that **everything inside an application could be a stream,** and in a certain way it's exactly what the reactive paradigm is leveraging: we can transform listeners with callbacks in event streams, we can wrap an http request in a stream and handle the response by manipulating the data before updating a view, and we can use streams as communication channels for passing data between two or more objects, and many other use cases.

In the reactive panorama we need to introduce a particular type of stream: **the observable**.

A great definition of observable is available on the Rx.JS 5 documentation:

An Observable is a lazily evaluated computation that can synchronously or asynchronously return zero to (potentially) infinite values from the time it's invoked onwards. (http://bit.ly/2sWVEAf)

In order to consume data emitted by an observable, we need to create an observer (*consumer*); this subscribes to the observable and reacts every time a value is emitted by the observable (*producer*).

If we want to summarize in technical words what an observable is, we could say that an observable is an object that wrap some data consumed by an observer (an object with a specific contract) and once instantiated provides a cancellation function.

The observer is an object that allows us to retrieve the value emitted by an observable and has a specific contract exposing three methods: **next, error, and complete functions**.

When you deal with observables and observers bear in mind two well-known design patterns for fully understand their mechanisms: the observer and the iterator patterns.

Observer Pattern

The Observer Pattern is a behavioral pattern where an object called Subject maintains a list of other objects (*observers*) that want to be notified when a change happens inside the program.

The observers are usually subscribing to a change and then every time they receive a notification, they verify internally if they need to handle the notification or not.

Usually, in typed languages, the Observer Pattern is composed by a subject and one or multiple observers.

The subject is handling the subscription, unsubscription, and the notification to an observer; then each observer implements a specific interface that contains a publish method (update) for reacting to a notification originated by another object or a user interaction and shared through the Subject (Figure 3-4).

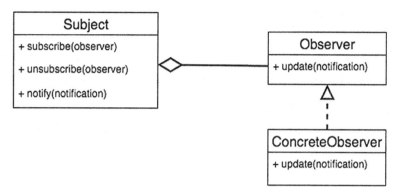

Figure 3-4. *Observer Pattern UML*

Iterator Pattern

The Iterator Pattern is a behavioral pattern used for traversing a data container like an array or an object, for instance.

As JavaScript developers, we should be familiar with this pattern, considering it was added in ECMAScript 2015.

This pattern allows an object to be traversed calling a method (next) for retrieving a subsequent value from the current one if it exists. The iterator pattern usually exposes the next method and the hasNext method that returns a Boolean used for checking if the object traversed contains more values or not.

In MDN we can find more information about the official JavaScript implementation in ECMAScript 2015: https://mzl.la/2sfrMxJ (Figure 3-5).

Figure 3-5. *Iterator Pattern UML*

Putting the Code into Practice

Let's create an example by walking through the code for a better understanding of how an observable/observer relation works in practice:

```
const observable = Observable.range(1, 10);
const observer = observable.subscribe(onData, onError, onComplete);
function onData(value){
        console.log(value);
}
function onError(err){
        console.error(err);
}
function onComplete(){
        console.log("stream complete!");
}
```

As you can see from this first example in the first line we have created an observable that contains a range of values from 1 to 10; that means we have these values ready to be emitted to an observer when the observer will subscribe to it.

On the second line we subscribe to the observable; the subscribe method in many libraries has three parameters that correspond to callbacks called once the observable is emitting a value, an error, or a complete signal.

In the rest of the code we are just reacting to the information emitted by the observable printing to the console an output that could be either an event from the stream or an error or the complete signal.

When an observable receives events can also allow us to manipulate the data for providing a different output from them like we have seen previously in the marble diagram where we were mapping each single value emitted, increasing by 1 each of them.

Different Reactive libraries are providing different sets of utilities, but the most complete one when the book was written is without any doubt Rx.js. This library provides a set of operators for manipulating not only the events emitted by the observable but also with other observables; it is not unusual to transform observable of observables in flat observables: think about them as an array of arrays. These operators will allow us to flat the object nesting accessing directly to the values in the observables without the iteration complexity.

We are going to see the possibilities offered by operators in the next section when we explore the different Reactive libraries so we can understand in practice how to use it and what we can do with them. Obviously, we will review only the most used ones because there are literally hundreds and our focus is on understanding the mechanism behind them more than exploring the entire library.

Stream Implementations

Now that we understood what streams are, it's time to get a better understanding of what is available in the front-end reactive ecosystem. The first library we are going to take into consideration is Rx.JS 5.

Rx.JS

Rx.JS is the most famous and used reactive library at the moment; it's used almost everywhere, from Angular 2 where the library is integrated inside the framework to many other smaller or larger frameworks that are embracing this library and leveraging its power.

It's one of the most complete reactive libraries with many operators and a great documentation, Rx.JS is part of Reactive Extensions (`http://reactivex.io`). Learning it will mean being able to switch from one language to another using the same paradigm and often the same APIs.

Rx.JS can be used on front-end applications as well on back-end ones with Node.js; obviously its asynchronous nature will help out on both sides of an application's development.

There are two main versions available. Version 4 is the first JavaScript porting of the Reactive Extension, and then recently another implementation started to rise up that is version 5. The two libraries have several differences in our examples and so we will use version 5.

In this section, we won't be able to play with all the operators available on Rx.JS because this library is broad enough for having its own book (in fact, there are many books available that I strongly suggest you give a go). Our main aim is to grasp a few key concepts, considering we are going to use it in many other examples in this and the next chapters.

Therefore we are going to see Rx.JS in action in three different scenarios:

- When we need to reduce our data for retrieving a final value.

- When we retrieve data from an HTTP endpoint.

- When we need to communicate with multiple objects via observables.

Considering how large Rx.JS is, we introduce another important concept such as the difference between hot and cold observables, to help to understand better how the other libraries work.

Let's start with a simple example on reducing an array of data and retrieve the sum of values filtering the duplicates present in the initial array.

```
import Rx from "rxjs"

const data = [1,2,10,1,3,9,6,13,11,10,10,3,19,18,17,15,4,8,4];

const onData = (value) => console.log(`current sum is ${value}`);
const onError = _ => console.log("stream error");
const onComplete = _ => console.log("stream completed");

const obs = Rx.Observable.from(data)
                          .filter(value => value % 2 === 0)
                          .distinct()
                          .reduce((acc, value) => acc + value);

obs.subscribe(onData, onError, onComplete);
```

As you can see in the example above, we are converting an array of numbers to an observable (Rx.Observable.from(data)), then we start to transform the values inside the array step by step, applying multiple transformations.

In fact, first we are filtering the values creating a new array containing only the even numbers, then we remove all the duplicates inside the array with the distinct operator provided by Rx.JS; and finally we sum the values inside the array with the reduce operator.

Figure 3-6 shows the final output in the browser console.

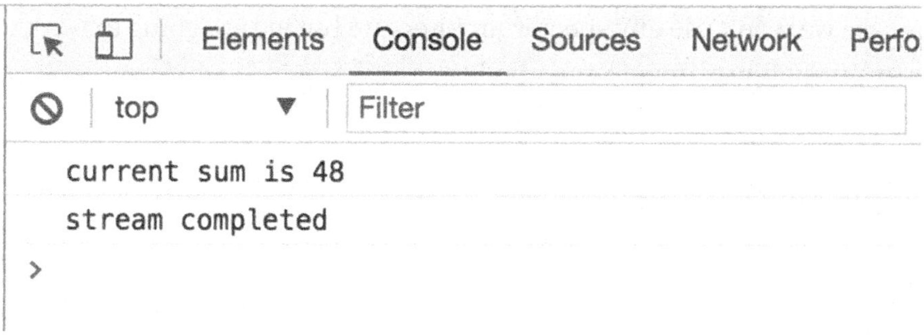

Figure 3-6. *Final result returned by the previous snippet with Rx.JS*

Every time we are applying a transformation via an operator, we are creating a new observable that is returned at the end of the operation.

This means we can concatenate multiple operators by applying several transformations to the same data source.

In order to output the final result of our observable, we are subscribing to the observable with the subscribe method, and this method accepts three functions. The first one is triggered every time the observable emits data, the second one if the observable emits an error, and the last one is triggered once the observable receives a complete signal from the producer (in our case, the end of the array).

Remember that these callbacks are not all mandatory; we can potentially skip to declare the error and complete callbacks if we don't need to react to these events.

Imagine for a moment how you would implement the same logic in imperative programming... done it?

Ok, now you probably understood how functional and reactive paradigms can help to express complex operations in few lines of code, having a clear idea of what's happening, without storing temporary values anywhere, and without generating any side effects. Everything is contained inside the observables and cannot be modified from external operations.

The next example, instead, aims to retrieve the response from an API on the Web and then propagate the result to a hypothetical view.

In this case we won't use any specific architecture but we are going to work well with the single responsibility principle and good encapsulation.

```
import Rx from "rxjs";

const URL = "https://jsonplaceholder.typicode.com/users";

const simplifyUserData = (user) => {
    return {
        name: user.name,
        email: user.email,
        website: user.website
    }
}

const intervalObs = Rx.Observable.interval(1000)
                                .take(2)
                                .mergeMap(_ => fetch(URL))
                                .mergeMap(data => data.json())
                                .mergeAll()
                                .map(simplifyUserData)

intervalObs.subscribe(user => {
    console.log(`user name is ${user.name}`);
    console.log(`user email is ${user.email}`);
    console.log(`user website is ${user.website}`);
    console.log('-----------------------------');
},
error => console.error("error", error),
complete => console.log("completed"))
```

After creating the constant with the URL to consume, we are creating a method (simplifyUserData) for filtering the data we want to use in our application, by just returning a subset of the information instead of the entire record retrieved from that URL.

The endpoint used is a public endpoint usually used for mocking data, but in our case we are going to receive an array of objects that looks like this:

```
{
  id: 1,
  name: "Leanne Graham",
  username: "Bret",
  email: "Sincere@april.biz",
  address: {
    street: "Kulas Light",
    suite: "Apt. 556",
    city: "Gwenborough",
    zipcode: "92998-3874"
[....]
}
```

We want to consume this endpoint every second but only twice during the application life cycle.

In order to do that we create an observable with an interval of a second (Rx.Observable.interval), specifying how many times we want to perform this operation (take operator) and then we want to fetch the data from a URL (first mergeMap) and then return the data fetched as JSON, splitting the object retrieved (mergeAll operator, we could have use other operators like concatAll, for instance, obtaining the same result) in order to emit a value per time instead of the entire array in one go. Finally we simplify the data with the method we created at the beginning of the script (map operator).

The final output of this example should look like Figure 3-7.

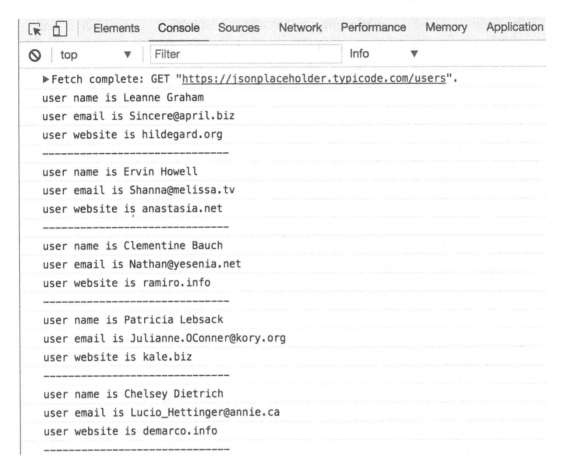

Figure 3-7. *Output of previous example with Rx.JS*

Now we need to understand in depth why we have done all these operations for manipulating the data to get the result displayed in the screenshot above.

After creating the interval observable, we perform at each tick a fetch operation. Fetch is not an observable but, as you can see from the example, we are not transforming it via an operator for translating it to an observable, but we are using the operator mergeMap and inside there we are performing the fetch operation.

- This is because fetch is a Promise A+ and these promises are recognized by Rx.JS, so without the need of using the fromPromise operators like the standard promises, we can use them straightaway inside our Observable created by the mergeMap operator.

- `MergeMap` is an operator that is doing two things. The first one is merging two streams in a unique one and then iterating with the values emitted inside the streams: in this case it's flatting the promise in order to return just a stream with the service response.

- The second `mergeMap` operator is used with another promise and we are specifying the return value emitted in that stream should be the JSON representation of the data fetched from the endpoint.

- This second promise is due to the fetch API contract as you can see in the MDN specifications: `http://bit.ly/2sWVEAf`.

- The last operator is the `mergeAll` one, which usually should be used for merging all the observables inside an observable of observables, but in this case, it is flatting the last promise containing the array with the data retrieved and emitting each single value of the array in an iterative way instead of emitting the entire array as a unique value, allowing us to use the final operator (`map`) for simplifying the data emitted.

- It's easy to understand how versatile and powerful Rx.JS could be in a situation like this one. Obviously at this stage we know that there is some work to do to get familiar with all the different operators offered by Rx.JS, but don't be too sad because it's a step we all have done before mastering the reactive paradigm.

- Before reviewing another chunk of code, we need to explain another key concept of the observables: what it means when an observable is hot or cold.

Hot and Cold Observables

We can have two different types of observables: hot and cold.

A cold observable is lazy and unicast by nature; it starts to emit values only when someone subscribes to it.

Instead, the hot observables could emit events also before someone is listening without the need to wait for a trigger for starting its actions; also they are multicast by design.

Another important characteristic that we should understand for recognizing hot and cold observables is to understand how the producer is handled in both scenarios.

In cold observables, the producer lives inside the observable itself; therefore every time we subscribe to a cold observable, the producer is created again and again.

Instead, in the hot observable the producer is unique and shared across multiple observers; therefore we will receive fresh values every time we are subscribing to it without receiving all of them since the first value emitted. Obviously, there are ways in hot observables to create a buffer of values to emit every time an observer is subscribing to it, but we are not going to evaluate each single scenario right now.

Let's see a hot and a cold observable in action for having a better understanding of how to use these two types of objects using Rx.JS.

Cold Observables

The best way to understand a cold observable is seeing it in action:

```
import Rx from "rxjs";

const source = Rx.Observable.interval(2000).startWith(123)

source.subscribe(value => console.log("first observer", value))

setTimeout(_ =>{
    source.subscribe(value => console.log("second observer", value))
}, 5000);

setTimeout(_ =>{
    source.subscribe(value => console.log("third observer", value))
}, 8000)
```

The output of this small example is shown in Figure 3-8.

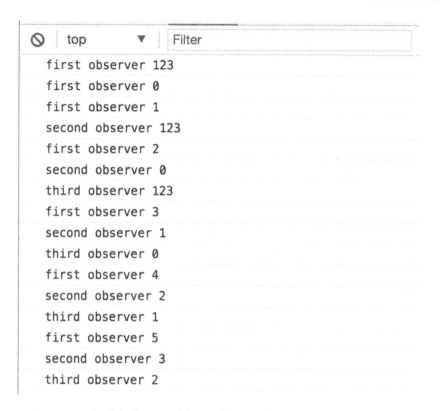

Figure 3-8. *Output of cold observable with Rx.JS*

In this example we are creating an observable that is emitting a sequential value every 2 seconds: it will start from 0 until infinite because we didn't specify how many values we want to emit before the event streams is completed.

We use the `startWith` operator when we want to show an initial value in our user interface or to start a sequence of events without waiting for the values passed asynchronously.

In a cold observable we have the producer, in this case the observable emitting sequential numbers, which is instantiated three times – basically any time a consumer is subscribing to it. In the image above you can clearly see the sequence of numbers is starting every time a consumer is subscribing to the producer.

We can conclude that the cold observable re-instantiates the producer any time a consumer is subscribing and it is unicast so the values produced are listened by a consumer per time; also we can have multiple consumers subscribing to the same producer.

By default all the observables we create in Rx.JS are cold but we have different ways for transforming them into hot observables.

Hot Observables

Let's see what a hot observable looks like:

```
import Rx from "rxjs";

const source = Rx.Observable.interval(2000)
                        .startWith(123)
                        .publish()
                        .refCount();

source.subscribe(value => console.log("first observer", value))

setTimeout(_ =>{
    source.subscribe(value => console.log("second observer", value))
}, 5000);

setTimeout(_ =>{
    source.subscribe(value => console.log("third observer", value))
}, 8000)
```

The output is shown in Figure 3-9. The example is very similar to the cold observable one, but in this case we are using other two operators: publish and refCount.

Figure 3-9. *Output of hot observable with Rx.JS*

Publish operator is useful to transform our cold observables to hot observables because it returns a ConnectableObservable instead and observable object.

A ConnectableObservable starts emitting values only when a connect method is called or, like in our example, when we use refCount operator.

RefCount operator is used when we don't need to control the start and stop of the ConnectableObservable but instead we automate this process; when a consumer subscribes to a ConnectableObservable, it is the logic provided by refCount that will trigger the connect method for emitting the values to the subscribers.

Also the refCount logic will unsubscribe once there are any subscribers ready for receiving new values.

When we have a hot observable the producer becomes multicast and the values emitted are shared across all the subscribers but at the same time we need to remember that by default, it's not waiting for any consumer to subscribe. Instead it is emitting values immediately after the connect method is called.

There are operators that will allow you to control when a hot observable starts to emit values like `multicast` and `connect` instead of `refCount,` which is automating these steps. Just keep this in mind when you work with Rx.JS because there are many opportunities available with this great library so keep an eye on the documentation and the implementation will become very smooth.

Understanding what we are subscribing to and what are the characteristics and benefits of a hot or a cold observable could save a lot of debugging time and many headaches once our code hits the production stage.

I think it is clear that Rx.JS is not just that – it's way more than that but with these simple examples we are trying to memorize a few useful key concepts that will facilitate the integration of this library in our existing or new applications.

Now it's time to see another reactive library flavor with XStream. It's important to understand that the concepts showed in the Rx.JS sections are very similar in other libraries; therefore owning them will allow you to pick the right library for the a project.

XStream

XStream is one of the most recent reactive libraries created by André Staltz for providing a simple way to approach reactive programming tailored specifically for Cycle.js.

XStream leverages a few concepts that we have already seen in action with Rx.JS like the observables but by simplifying the core concepts behind streams. All the streams are hot observables and there isn't a way to create cold observables with this library.

I personally think the author took into consideration the reactive programming learning curve when he worked on this library, and he tried smoothing out the entry level in order to be more approachable by newbies and experts as well.

On top, XStream is very fast, second only to Most.js (another reactive library), and very light too, around 30kb; and with less than 30 operators available, it represents a super basic library for dealing with observables, perfect for any prototype or project that requires the use of observables but without all the "commodities" offered by other libraries with plenty of operators.

XStream is using instead of observables the **streams** concepts, which are event emitters with multiple listeners. A **listener** is an object with a specific contract, and it has three public methods: next, error, and complete; as the name suggests, a listener object is listening to events emitted by a stream.

Comparing streams and listeners to Rx.JS observables and observers, we can say that a stream is acting like a hot observable and the listener like an observer mimicking the same implementation.

Last but not least, in XStream we can use **producers** for generating events broadcasted via a stream to multiple objects. The producer controls the life cycle of the stream emitting the values at its convenience. A producer has a specific signature, and it exposes two main methods: start and stop. We will see later an example that will introduce the producer concept.

Now it's time to see XStream in action, porting the examples we have approached previously during the Rx.JS section.

The first example is related to reducing an array of values that extracts just the even numbers, removing the duplicates and calculating their sum:

```
import xs from 'xstream';

const data = [1,2,10,1,3,9,6,13,11,10,10,3,19,18,17,15,4,8,4];

const filterEven = (value) => value % 2 === 0;
const removeDuplicates = (inputStream) => {
    const buffer = [];
    const outputStream = xs.fromArray(buffer);
    inputStream.addListener({
        next(value){
            if(buffer.length === 0 || buffer.indexOf(value) < 0)
                buffer.push(value);
        }
    })
    return outputStream;
}
const sumValues = (acc, value) => acc + value;

const listener = {
    next(value){
        console.log(`current sum is ${value}`);
    },
    error(){
        console.error("stream error");
    },
```

```
   complete(){
       console.log("stream completed");
   }
}

const stream = xs.fromArray(data)
                  .filter(filterEven)
                  .compose(removeDuplicates)
                  .fold(sumValues, 0);

stream.addListener(listener);
```

The data object contains an array of unordered integers with duplicates values and even and odd numbers. Our aim for this exercise is to filter the array retrieving only the even numbers, removing the duplicates after the first transformation, and finally calculating the final sum.

After instantiating the array source, we are defining the transformation we are going to apply; the first one is filtering the even numbers from the initial array with the method filterEven.

In this method we are checking that each value we are going to receive is divisible by 2 or not. If so it means the value is an even number so we want to keep it, otherwise we will skip it (remember that a stream will emit 1 value per time).

The second method is removeDuplicates, but in XStream there isn't an operator for doing it automatically like for Rx.JS. As we said at the beginning, XStream is meant for learning how to handle streams more than having a complete library with many operators.

Therefore we are going to use the compose operator that returns a stream and expects a new stream as input. OutputStream will be our new stream used by the next operator emitting the array generated inside the removeDuplicates method.

Inside removeDuplicates we create an array for storing the unique values and we push them only if are not present inside the array.

The last transformation for this exercise is calculating the sum of the values filtered in the previous steps. We are going to use the fold operator that requests a function with two arguments: an accumulator and the current value to evaluate for calculating the final result, very similar to the reduce method used when you wanted to calculate the values inside an array.

Finally, we can create the stream using `xs.fromArray` passing the initial array, and this will produce an initial stream that will emit the array values. After that we apply all the different transformations via XStream operators like filter, compose, and fold. Bear in mind that the second parameter of the fold operator is the accumulator initial value, and in our case we want to start from the value zero and sum all the others.

The last step is to listen to the stream creating a listener. As we said at the beginning of this section, a listener is just an object with a specific signature (next, error, complete), and in our case we output to the console the transformation made inside our stream. Opening the dev tools of your favorite browser, you should see something like Figure 3-10.

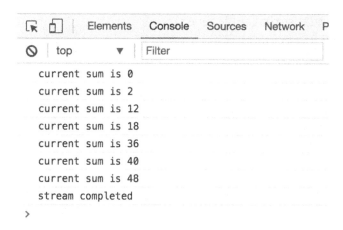

Figure 3-10. *Output of XStream example, slightly different from the Rx.JS example due to the fold operator*

As we can see, this example made with XStream resembles the one we did previously with Rx.JS. The key takeaway here is the fact that understanding how the observables work are helping us to switch from a reactive library to another one without investing time on learning new concepts but just applying a few basic concepts with different syntax and operators.

Our second example is based on retrieving some data from a REST endpoint every few seconds.

In this case we can leverage the power of the producer objects available in XStream for fetching the remote data and emitting the result to a stream.

Considering we want to retrieve the data every few seconds for a certain amount of times, we can use an interval stream instead of a set interval like we would do in plain JavaScript.

This is our code example:

```
import xs from "xstream";
import fetch from "fetch";
const URL = "https://jsonplaceholder.typicode.com/users";

const producer = {
    emitter(){
        const that = this;
        return {
            next(){
                emitUserData(listener);
            },
            complete(){
                that.stop()
            }
        }
    },
    start(listener){
        xs.periodic(5000).take(2).addListener(this.emitter())
    },
    stop(){
        listener.complete();
    }
}

const emitUserData = (listener) => {
    fetch.fetchUrl(URL, (error, meta, body) => {
        if(error) return;

        const data = JSON.parse(body.toString());
        data.forEach(user => {
            listener.next(user)
        }, this);
    })
}
```

```
const simplifyUserData = (user) => {
    return {
        name: user.name,
        email: user.email,
        website: user.website
    }
}

const listener = {
    next(user){
        console.log(`user name is ${user.name}`);
        console.log(`user email is ${user.email}`);
        console.log(`user website is ${user.website}`);
        console.log('-----------------------------');
    },
    error(){
        console.error("stream error");
    },
    complete(){
        console.log("stream completed");
    }
}

const userStream = xs.create(producer).map(simplifyUserData);
userStream.addListener(listener);
```

As you can see in the example above, we start defining our producer object; remember that a producer is just an object that requires two methods: start and stop. The start method will be called once the first consumer subscribes to the stream.

Keep in mind that a producer can have just one listener per time; therefore, in order to broadcast the results to multiple listeners, we have to create a stream that uses the producer to emit the values.

Our producer contains also another method called emitter that returns a listener object that we are going to use inside the interval stream created in the start method.

The start method uses the xs.periodic operator that accepts as an argument an interval of time when an event is emitted by the stream; so in our case, every 5 seconds a new event will be emitted.

We also used the operator take that is used for retrieving a certain amount of values from that stream, ignoring all the others emitted.

The last thing to do is to subscribe to that stream with a listener and every tick (next method) fetches the data from the endpoint.

The endpoint is the same one as the previous example in Rx.JS, so we need to expect the same JSON object fetched from the endpoint.

The main goal of this example is outputting a simplified version of this data that could be used in a hypothetical view of our application.

When we create simplifyUserData method for extracting only the information we need from the value emitted in the stream; this function is returning a filtered object containing only a few fields instead of the entire collection.

After that, we create our listener object with the typical signature next, error, and complete methods where we are handling the values emitted by the stream.

Finally, we create the glue between the stream and the listener object by creating a stream with xs.create passing as the argument our producer.

Then we iterate through all the values emitted, filtering the user data and in the last line of our script we associate the listener to the stream that will trigger the producer to start emitting the values.

In this case there are some differences compared to Rx.JS example but again the key concepts are still there.

The last example for the XStream library is focused on how we broadcast values to multiple listener objects; in this case XStream is helping us because all the streams are hot, therefore multicast by nature.

We don't need to perform any action or understand what kind of stream we are dealing with. That's also why I recommend always starting with a simple library like XStream that contains everything we need for getting our hands dirty with streams and then moving to a more complete toolbox library like Rx.JS or Most.js.

```
import xs from "xstream";

const periodicStream = xs.periodic(1000)
                        .map(_ => Math.floor(Math.random()*1000) + 100);
periodicStream.addListener({
    next(value){
```

```
        console.log("first listener", value);
    }
})

setTimeout(_ =>{
    periodicStream.addListener({
        next(value){
            console.log("second listener", value);
        }
    })
}, 3000);

setTimeout(_ =>{
    periodicStream.addListener({
        next(value){
            console.log("third listener", value);
        }
    })
}, 6000);
```

The first thing is to create a stream (`periodicStream` constant) that emits every second a random number.

Then every time we are adding a new listener to the main stream, each listener receives the value emitted by the `periodicStream`.

Checking the output on the browser's console we can see how the stream works; remember that we said any stream in XStream is a hot one and multicast. Therefore we will have just one producer that won't be re-created but every time a new listener is subscribing, we receive the value emitted from that moment onward (Figure 3-11).

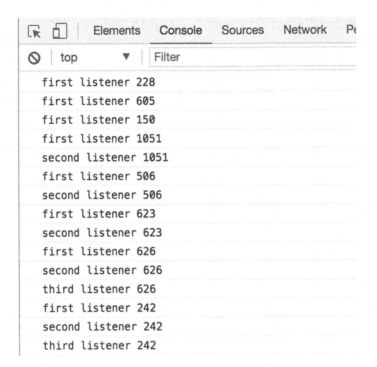

Figure 3-11. *Output XStream example with hot streams*

Now we can see we have the expected behavior, when the second and the third listener subscribe to the stream they receive the value emitted without any information of the previous values like we have seen in the cold observable example in Rx.JS.

From this last example it is clear that if you need to manage with a certain granularity the streams type in a project, Rx.JS would be the right choice for that. Otherwise XStream could simplify and speed up your development, considering that it is pretty straightforward.

Back Pressure

Another important Reactive Programming concept is backpressure and how we can use it for improving our reactive applications.

When we work with multiple streams, they could emit a large amount of events in a short period of time. Therefore we need a way for alleviating the amount of data consumed by the observers if we don't really need all of them or if the process to elaborate them is too computationally intense, and the consumer is not able to keep up.

Usually we have two possibilities to handle back pressure in our application: first, we can queue the value, creating a buffer and elaborate all the values received, so in this case we don't miss the values emitted. This strategy is called **loss-less strategy**.

Another strategy could be skipping some events and reacting only after a certain amount of time, filtering what we receive because maybe this information is not critical for what the consumer needs to do; in this case we call this strategy **lossy strategy.**

Imagine, for example, that we are merging two observables with a **zip operator**. The first observable is providing some capital case letters every second, and the second observable is emitting lowercase letters every 200 milliseconds.

The zip operator in this case will create a new observable with the values of the two streams coupled together, but because it needs to couple the letters from different streams that are emitting values with different speed, inside the zip operator we have a buffer for storing the values of the second observable until the first one is going to emit the following value.

Figure 3-12 should shed some light on our final goal.

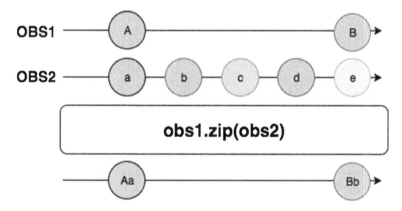

Figure 3-12. *Example of back pressure*

As you can see from the marble diagram above, the second stream is producing 5 times more values than the first one in the same amount of time, so the new observable will need to maintain the data in a buffer to match the values before emitting them to the consumer.

Unfortunately, these kinds of scenarios in Reactive Programming are not rare and in this occasion, back pressure operators come to the rescue.

These operators allow us to alleviate the pressure from the observer by simply stopping a reaction from values emitted by an observable, pausing the reception of values until we define when to resume receiving the values.

Let's write a concrete example with Rx.JS for understanding better the concept described.

What we are going to create with Rx.JS and React is a simple box with a simulation of a stock that receives data in real time and it needs to display the stock value inside the component (Figure 3-13).

Figure 3-13. *Outcome of our next exercise on back pressure*

This small example is composed by two files: the main application and the React component.

The main application will generate the observable that will produce random values in a specific range ready to be displayed inside the component.

```
import React from "react";
import ReactDOM from "react-dom";
import Rx from "rxjs";
import Stock from "./Stock.jsx";

export default class App{
    constructor(){
        const cont = document.getElementById("app");
        const observable = this.generateProducer();
        const AAPL = "AAPL - Apple Inc.";
        ReactDOM.render(<Stock producer$={observable} title={AAPL} />, cont);
    }
}
```

```
generateProducer(){
        const stockValuesProducer = Rx.Observable.interval(50)
.map(value => {
return (Math.random() * 50 + 100).toFixed(2);
})

        return stockValuesProducer;
    }
}

let app = new App();
```

What is happening in the main application file is that we are generating a producer (generateProducer method) that should simulate a constant interaction with a source of data, and every 50 milliseconds it is emitting a value between 100 and 150 with 2 decimals.

This is a typical example where the back pressure operators could help out; we really don't need to update the UI every 50 milliseconds because more than a useful experience, we are going to create a constant refresh that won't be well received by our users, and it will be very intensive, in particular, on low-end machines. So what can we do to alleviate the pressure on the observer that is going to receive these values?

If in generateProducer method, instead of returning the observable as it is, we could add a back pressure operator like this one:

```
generateProducer(){
        const stockValuesProducer = Rx.Observable.interval(50)
.map(value => {
return (Math.random() * 50 + 100).toFixed(2);
                                                    })

        return stockValuesProducer.sampleTime(500);
}
```

In this case, the sampleTime operator will emit a value only every 500 milliseconds, ignoring the other values received in the meantime.

Just to fix this concept even better, Figure 3-14 shows how this works inside a marble diagram.

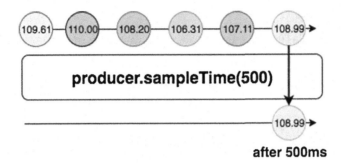

Figure 3-14. *Marble diagram showing sampleTIme operator with half-second debounce*

In the component code, we are going to subscribe to the observable received from the producer property and display the value in our UI:

```
import React from "react";

export default class Stock extends React.Component{
    constructor(){
        super();
        this.state = {stockValue: 0};
    }

    componentDidMount(){
        this.props.producer$.subscribe(this.setStockValue.bind(this));
    }

    setStockValue(value){
        this.setState({stockValue: value});
    }

    render(){
        return (
            <div className="stock">
                <h2>{this.props.title}</h2>
                <p>${this.state.stockValue}</p>
            </div>
        )
    }
}
```

As we can notice inside the `componentDidMount` method, provided by the React component life cycle, we are subscribing to the producer (the observable created before in the main application) and then we set the stock value in the React state object for displaying it in our paragraph element.

In Rx.JS we can use multiple back pressure operators like debounce or throttle, but there are many others for handling the back pressure properly. It's important to remember to not create a huge buffer of data when the producer is emitting a large amount of data. So as a rule of thumb, remember that when we don't need all the data emitted by an observable, we should really filter them for providing a better user experience to our users and improve the performance of our Reactive applications.

Wrap-Up

In this chapter, we explained how to work with a few key reactive concepts; in particular, we introduced the concepts of streams, observables and observers on Rx.JS and streams and listeners in XStream. We also reviewed the most famous libraries implementations and how we can use them in order to manipulate our streams.

We have discovered what and hot and cold observables are and how to handle the back pressure when we receive a large amount of data that we don't need to share all of inside our stream.

Now we have all the tools we need to see concrete implementation and how different frameworks/libraries introduced reactive programming in the front-end world.

Obviously, the aim of this book is not going in depth on each single operator or a specific library but providing the knowledge to jump from a library to another one without headaches.

There are also other libraries not mentioned in this chapter that could replace Rx.JS and XStream like, for instance, Most.js (`https://github.com/cujojs/most`) or IxJS (`https://github.com/ReactiveX/IxJS`) or Kefir (`https://rpominov.github.io/kefir/`) or FlyD (`https://github.com/paldepind/flyd`) or again Bacon.js (`https://baconjs.github.io/`).

All of them have their pros and cons and I strongly suggest taking a look at each single one as well as picking the right library for your projects.

In the next few chapters we are going to see Reactive programming in action. In particular we will explore Cycle.js and how this simple library is able to handle function reactive programming with its innovative architecture called MVI (Model-View-Intent). We then approach MobX, a library very famous in the reactive front-end world that is becoming more popular day by day and is solving the application state management in an easy and reactive way. We will finish this book with SAM Pattern, an architectural pattern that provides a reactive structure that is totally framework agnostic, giving us the possibility to integrate it in any existing or greenfield project.

CHAPTER 4

Cycle.js and MVI

We cannot solve our problems with the same thinking we used when we created them.

—Albert Einstein

In this chapter, we are introducing Cycle.js, a functional and reactive framework that is very interesting in the front-end panorama for the number of concepts ported from different languages and wired together from the knowledgeable mind of the creator and the Cycle community.

Cycle.js (cycle.js.org) was created by André Staltz, one of the most famous and active advocate of the front-end reactive panorama; in fact, André is a contributor of Rx.JS and the mind behind XStream library.

As we are going to see in the chapter, Cycle.js can be used in several ways. Its modularity guarantees great results in any project, providing a great level of encapsulation and enhancing the components' reusability across multiple projects without the need of "copying and pasting" part of a specific flow from different files like in other framework implementations.

Introduction to Cycle.js

The Cycle.js focus is on the interaction between computer and user, taking into consideration research on human-computer interaction and studies focused on the interfaces between human beings and computers.

This interaction is a circular one between the inputs and outputs as shown in Figure 4-1.

© Luca Mezzalira 2018
L. Mezzalira, *Front-End Reactive Architectures*, https://doi.org/10.1007/978-1-4842-3180-7_4

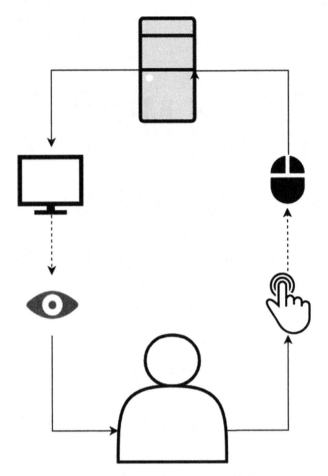

Figure 4-1. *Interaction schema between human and computer*

As we can see, a person can interact with a computer via its input methods (mouse, keyboard, microphone, touchpad...); for doing this, the person will use a hand or the voice as output.

When the computer receives the input from the user, it will elaborate a new output related to the input received, providing it on the screen.

The user then will be able to recognize and elaborate on the computer's output via the user's input sense (eyes or ears, for instance), understanding how his interactions affect the computer's output, creating de facto, a circular interaction between computer and user: from here, the name of Cycle.js.

We could summarize this interaction saying that between the human and the computer there is a dialogue where the two main actors are interacting with each other, reacting to the inputs and providing a new output.

As we understand, this framework uses a different approach from the others we used to work with where the GUI is at the center; instead Cycle.js privileges more the interactions aspect over the graphical representation.

In order to do that, Cycle.js introduces a **message passing architecture** where we send a message to an object and this one knows which part of the code to run based on the input received.

This highly decoupled architecture stands on the opposite edge of the spectrum compared to more traditional architectures where dependency injection is heavily used and we favor objects interactions over reactivity.

Cycle is not the only framework leveraging a message passing architecture; other examples could be retrieved in Akka with the actor-model architecture or in CSP (Communicating Sequential Processes) with channels.

During the chapter, we will discover that using this approach will lead Cycle. js projects to a better separation of concerns and encapsulation, in favor of better components reusability across projects.

But it's time to see Cycle in action though, so let's move to some concrete examples to truly appreciate the ideas behind this reactive framework.

Structuring a Simple Cycle.js Application

The first key concept we need to stick in our mind when we work with Cycle.js is the fact that this framework is clearly separating the application logic from the side effects.

For example, let's assume we want to load some data from an endpoint after the user clicks on a button in our interface.

Cycle.js separates completely the DOM rendering and the remote data fetching from the logic of preparing the HTTP request and the data manipulation to be presented in the DOM; in this way we can focus on what really matters inside our application delegating de facto the real action of manipulating the DOM or fetching remote data with a HTTPRequest object.

Before examining a simple Cycle application, we need to explore how this framework is composed.

In Cycle.js there are three key concepts to remember:

- Pure functions

- Streams

- Drivers

A **pure function** is a functional concept where a function can be defined as pure if it doesn't create side effects inside the program, so when we pass a specific parameter it always returns the same output. We could summarize the pure function concept as a function where its output is determined only by the input values, and an example could be:

```
function add(a, b){
        return a + b;
}
```

In this case when I call the function add I receive a result based on the function's arguments (a and b), and there is no possibility that external states or variables could affect the final result considering that our pure function is totally independent from the application where it is running.

Another key concept is the **stream**, but considering we extensively talked about them in the previous chapters we can move to the next concept: the **drivers.**

For better understanding the drivers, we need to analyze how Cycle.js is composed; otherwise we will struggle to catch why the drivers are used in this framework.

Cycle.js is a modular architecture composed of multiple libraries. The core library is really small and it exposes just one method used for creating the glue between the application logic and the side effects like a DOM state rendering or remote data connection.

By default, Cycle.js uses XStream as a main stream library but it allows us to use other libraries like Rx.JS, Most.js, or even a custom one created by us.

We have already discussed how Cycle.js separates the application logic from the side effects: this is the key part for understanding the drivers. All the side effects in a Cycle application are handled by drivers, for instance, one of the most used ones is the DOM driver that performs the DOM manipulation received by the application logic that instead prepares a virtual DOM representation instead of interacting directly with the DOM.

The communication between the drivers and the application is always made via observables; a driver can be a read and write or a read-only driver.

The rule of thumb here is that a driver has always as input an observable but may or may not return an output.

If we want to draw the anatomy of a Cycle application we could use this example as a skeleton:

```
import xs from 'xstream';
import {run} from '@cycle/run';
import {makeDOMDriver, p} from '@cycle/dom'

const main = sources => {
    const sinks = {
        DOM: xs.periodic(1000).map(v => p(`seconds: ${v}`))
    }
    return sinks;
}

const drivers = {
  DOM: makeDOMDriver('#app')
};

run(main, drivers);
```

Let's analyze what we have in this basic example.

After importing XStream, Cycle run function, and the DOMDriver, all the Cycle.js applications have a run function; a pure function, composed by a sources object; and a sink object as output that contains the logic for the side effects to be applied after our application finishes the elaboration.

For instance, in this example we have a stream that every second is incrementing a variable and returning a virtual DOM, in this case a virtual paragraph object.

Taking a look at the DOM driver, we can see that as a parameter of the DOMDriver method we need to pass the HTML element to use for appending our future DOM elements created dynamically by our Cycle.js application.

The last, but essential, thing to do is calling the method run provided by the framework for creating the glue between the main function and the drivers.

What the run method is doing is simple to explain; this method is creating a circular dependency between the main function and the drivers retrieving the output of each function and returning as a source of the other as we explained at the beginning of this chapter.

Obviously the input and output are always object-containing observables and it's where Cycle is really shining with its architecture.

An important piece of information that we didn't mention before is related to the virtual DOM library used in Cycle.js.

Cycle uses Snabbdom (`http://bit.ly/2gtpUKP`) out of the box, a JavaScript library leveraging similar concepts expressed in React.js like the Virtual DOM and good diffing algorithm, on top Snabbdom offers a modular and minimal implementation compared to React (only 200 lines of code).

Performance wise, Snabbdom results faster and more performant than React.js version 15 and below; it's heavily based on function and could be used with JSX syntax with Babel if we are familiar with React.js.

Snabbdom would require another chapter for explaining in depth the beauty of this Virtual DOM library, but because it's not the main topic of this chapter we can get more information with these resources:

Snabbdom on github: `http://bit.ly/2gtpUKP`

Snabbdom JSX: `http://bit.ly/2wxqDSE`

React-less Virtual DOM with Snabbdom: `http://bit.ly/1QFVayF`

Now let's try to see a more complete example where we are going to create a simple weather forecast application that allows the user to search for a specific city and retrieve the weather forecasts for the next five days, and the UI looks like Figure 4-2.

Figure 4-2. Cycle.js Project UI

This example will follow us for the entire chapter and we will refine it with two different approaches in order to explore properly the different possibilities offered by Cycle.js.

Let's start to list what we need to do in order to create the weather application with Cycle.js:

- We need to use two drivers: one for the DOM manipulation and another one for fetching the data from a remote REST service.

- We need to create an input field with a button that will allow the user to search for a specific city.

- We need to request the data to render to a weather forecast service (in this case a third-party service).

- We need to create our UI with a title on the top, the current day forecast highlighted, and a list of the following days.

The first thing to create is the typical Cycle skeleton application with a `run` method, the drivers. and the `main` function:

```
const main = sources => {
    // here there will be our application logic
}
const drivers = {
  DOM: makeDOMDriver('#app'),
  HTTP: makeHTTPDriver()
};

run(main, drivers);
```

As planned, we have a DOM driver (`makeDOMDriver`) that will manipulate the DOM inside the div with id `app` and the HTTP driver that instead will perform the request to the weather forecast's endpoint.

That means in our main function we are going to return an object with two observables: one for the endpoint request providing which city the user is interested on, and one with the virtual DOM of our page. Then the drivers will take care to perform the actions for us.

Let's go ahead creating our application view, for instance, if we want to create the input field with the button shown in the application picture presented before, we need to create a function called getForm that will return to us the virtual DOM version of our elements:

```
const getForm = () => div(".form", [
    input("#location-input"),
    button("#location-btn", "get forecasts")
])
```

Now we can observe for changes happening in both interactive elements in order to capture the text inserted by the user in the input field and when the user clicks the button for retrieving the forecast.

In order to do that we are going to add these few lines in our main function:

```
const input$ = sources.DOM.select("#location-input").events("focusout")
                              .map(evt => evt.target.value);
const btn$ = sources.DOM.select("#location-btn").events("mousedown");
```

Remember that everything can be a stream when we work with reactive programming; therefore once the driver will render our interactive elements in the real DOM, it will provide us access to the real DOM available in the DOM object and we are able to observe the user interactions, thanks to the APIs provided by the DOM driver.

Every time the user will click the button we will need to retrieve what he typed and prepare the request URL and the query string for allowing the HTTP driver to perform the real request.

Because we need to react when the user clicks the button but also to understand what the user wrote in the input field, we are going to combine the two streams in a unique one, and we prepare the URL with the new parameters any time the producer is producing new values, so in the main function we will add:

```
const merged$ = xs.combine(input$, btn$);
const request$ = merged$.map(([city, mouseEvt]) => getRequest(city))
                    .startWith(getRequest(INIT_CITY))
```

And we then create getRequest function that returns the composed URL:

```
const getRequest = city => {
    return {
        url: `http://api.apixu.com/v1/forecast.json?key=04ca1fa2705645e4830
        214415172307&q=${city}&days=7`,
        category: CATEGORY
    }
}
```

The request$ stream will be the one that we are going to pass to the HTTP driver, and this one will perform the real HTTP request for us, as you can see Cycle is separating the application logic from the side effect, defining what the application should do from how to perform the real effect.

In the combined stream, we can spot that there is a startWith method that returns a default city, in our case London, just for providing some information to the user the first time that accesses our weather application and he didn't interact with our input field yet.

It's time to handle the response once the HTTP driver receives it; inside our main function again we are going to retrieve the HTTP object exposed by the driver, and we are going to prepare the data for a set of functions for generating the virtual DOM based on the data retrieved by the HTTP driver.

```
const response$ = sources.HTTP.select(CATEGORY)
                                .flatten()

const vdom$ = response$.map(parseResponse)
                       .map(simplifyData)
                       .map(generateVDOM)
                       .startWith(h1("Loading..."))
```

And outside our main function we then create the functions needed for generating the UI:

```
const parseResponse = response => JSON.parse(response.text);
const simplifyData = data => {
                                return {
                                    city: data.location.name,
                                    current: data.current,
                                    forecast: data.forecast.forecastday
```

```
                            }
                        }
const generateVDOM = data => div(".main-container", [
        h1(`Your forecasts for ${data.city}`),
        getForm(),
        generateCurrentForecast(data.current),
        generateNext5Days(data.forecast)
    ])
```

As you can see in the main function, once we receive the response we need to select which one we handle, in this case the CATEGORY one described at the beginning of our application. Then we need to flatten the result because the HTTP driver returns always a stream of streams, so if we want to manipulate the data in this complex structure we need to create a flat stream (flatten method).

For creating the virtual DOM that will be passed to the DOM driver, we need now to do the following:

1. Parse the response and return a JSON object (parseResponse method).

2. Extract only the data our UI needs in order to render the final result (simplifyData method).

3. Generate the virtual DOM passing the elaborated data (generateVDOM method).

These three operations are generating a final stream with the virtual DOM that will be rendered via the DOM driver.

The last bit of our main function is what it returns, so a sink object containing a stream for the DOM driver and one for the HTTP driver that represent the output of our Cycle application.

This is the final implementation of our first Cycle example:

```
import xs from 'xstream';
import {run} from '@cycle/run';
import {makeDOMDriver, div, h1, h2, h3, img, p, input, button} from
'@cycle/dom';
import {makeHTTPDriver} from '@cycle/http';
```

```
import debounce from 'xstream/extra/debounce'
import moment from 'moment';

const CATEGORY = "forecast";
const INIT_CITY = "London";

const getForm = () => div(".form", [
    input("#location-input"),
    button("#location-btn", "get forecasts")
])

const generateNext5Days = forecasts => {
    const list = forecasts.map(forecast => {
        return div(".forecast-box", [
            h3(moment(forecast.date).format("dddd Do MMM")),
            p(`min ${forecast.day.mintemp_c}°C - max ${forecast.day.
            maxtemp_c}°C`),
            img(".forecast-img", {
                props: {
                    src: `http:${forecast.day.condition.icon}`
                }
            }),
            p(".status", forecast.day.condition.text)
        ])
    });
    return div(".forecasts-container", list)
}
const generateCurrentForecast = forecast => div(".current-forecast-
container", [
    div(".today-forecast", [
            img(".forecast-img", {
                props: {
                    src: `http:${forecast.condition.icon}`
                }
            }),
            p(".status", forecast.condition.text)
        ]),
```

```
        h3(moment(forecast.last_updated).format("dddd Do MMMM YYYY")),
        h2(`${forecast.temp_c}°C`),
        p(`humidity: ${forecast.humidity}%`)
    ])

const parseResponse = response => JSON.parse(response.text);
const simplifyData = data => {
                            return {
                                city: data.location.name,
                                current: data.current,
                                forecast: data.forecast.forecastday
                            }
                        }
const generateVDOM = data => div(".main-container", [
        h1(`Your forecasts for ${data.city}`),
        getForm(),
        generateCurrentForecast(data.current),
        generateNext5Days(data.forecast)
    ])

const getRequest = city => {
    return {
        url: `http://api.apixu.com/v1/forecast.json?key=04ca1fa2705645e4830
        214415172307&q=${city}&days=7`,
        category: CATEGORY
    }
}

const main = sources => {
    const input$ = sources.DOM.select("#location-input").events("focusout")
                            .map(evt => evt.target.value);
    const btn$ = sources.DOM.select("#location-btn").events("mousedown");
    const merged$ = xs.combine(input$, btn$);
    const request$ = merged$.map(([city, mouseEvt]) => getRequest(city))
                            .startWith(getRequest(INIT_CITY))

    const response$ = sources.HTTP.select(CATEGORY)
                                    .flatten()
```

```
    const vdom$ = response$.map(parseResponse)
                          .map(simplifyData)
                          .map(generateVDOM)
                          .startWith(h1("Loading..."))

    return {
        DOM: vdom$,
        HTTP: request$
    }
}

const drivers = {
  DOM: makeDOMDriver('#app'),
  HTTP: makeHTTPDriver()
};

run(main, drivers);
```

It's important to highlight a couple of things in this example. First of all, in our main function we are handling the input and the output of our application; we are not operating any real side effects that, instead, are delegated to the drivers.

The drivers and the main applications are communicating via streams; remember that Cycle.js is a message passing architecture, and this approach facilitates the data flow of our applications maintaining a high separation between application logic and side effects and a strong encapsulation.

For the first time in this book, we are looking to a reactive implementation where the communication between different parts of our architecture are made by streams; interestingly there isn't any knowledge in our application on how a driver is going to handle the side effects and we are not calling any specific method exposed by a driver. There is just a **circular dependency between our main function and the driver** that communicates only via streams.

It's important to iterate again these concepts because they will become very useful from now on considering we are going to discover MVI (model view intent), a reactive architecture heavily based on them.

Model View Intent Architecture

If you are familiar with ELM language and its architecture, MVI won't surprise you at all, but we need to admit that this is definitely a great improvement from the architecture we used in the past and in other famous frameworks like Redux or Angular.

But first, let's see what the Model View Intent is and how it differs from the other frameworks.

The first characteristic of this architecture is that it follows the unidirectional flow like the Flux pattern introduced by Facebook right after React.js, unidirectional flow is becoming a constant in many front-end reactive architectures.

What it means is that the data flow is always going in a unique direction and it never changes; this helps the debugging of your application and the possibility of adding new team members without a long induction period for explaining how the architecture of your applications work or how the system works.

FLUX PATTERN

Flux is a pattern introduced by Facebook that forces a monodirectional communication flow in web applications (Figure 4-3).

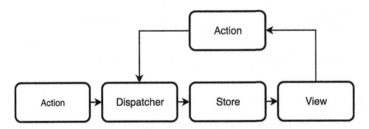

Figure 4-3. *Flux data flow diagram*

As you can see from the schema above, every time the user interacts with an element in the view, this one dispatches an action that is caught by a global dispatcher. The main aim of the dispatcher is triggering the callbacks the stores have registered in order to listen for the actions they are interested in. Once the store receives the data from the action performed, the changes needed for the view emit a change event to the view that will retrieve the data from the store and then they will render the changes updating the components' stated.

For more information visit: `http://bit.ly/2rHN8FO`.

Another characteristic we mentioned previously is the fact that the communication between Models Views and Intents happens via streams only; therefore there isn't any direct control between different modules but just a stream as input and one as output, like we have seen in the communication between Cycle.js application logic and drivers.

MVI is composed of three main modules:

- The **model** where we elaborate the user interactions and we keep the application state.

- The **view** where we wire our UI with the state provided by the model.

- The **intent** where we subscribe to user interactions or inputs and we provide them to the model for changing the state to a new one.

Figure 4-4 shows this architecture.

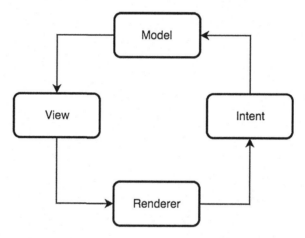

Figure 4-4. *MVI data flow diagram*

The renderer part represents the DOM driver in this case.

Let's see now how we can change our simple Cycle.js example using model view intent architecture.

The code we are going to explore is very similar to the previous example, so we will highlight only the key parts without investing too much time on how we have parsed the data retrieved from the HTTP driver or how we compose the virtual DOM elements rendered later on by the DOM driver.

The first thing to do is to identify in our previous example the part in our main function that should be allocated to different parts of an MVI architecture.

Originally our main function was implemented in the following way:

```
const main = sources => {
    const input$ = sources.DOM.select("#location-input").events("focusout")
                            .map(evt => evt.target.value);
    const btn$ = sources.DOM.select("#location-btn").events("mousedown");
    const merged$ = xs.combine(input$, btn$);
    const request$ = merged$.map(([city, mouseEvt]) => getRequest(city))
                        .startWith(getRequest(INIT_CITY))

    const response$ = sources.HTTP.select(CATEGORY)
                                .flatten()

    const vdom$ = response$.map(parseResponse)
                            .map(simplifyData)
                            .map(generateVDOM)
                            .startWith(h1("Loading..."))

    return {
        DOM: vdom$,
        HTTP: request$
    }
}
```

We can immediately identify the intent part in the first few lines of our implementation. As we said with the intent we are capturing the user intentions, therefore all the DOM interactions.

In fact, the intent receives as input the real DOM after being rendered and as output the user intentions as streams:

```
const intent = DOM => {
    const input$ = DOM.select("#location-input").events("focusout")
                            .map(evt => evt.target.value);
    const btn$ = DOM.select("#location-btn").events("mousedown");

    return xs.combine(input$, btn$)
                .map(([city, mouseEvt])=> getRequest(city))
                .startWith(getRequest(INIT_CITY))
}
```

The stream with the request will be passed to the model and to the HTTP driver for executing the request to the remote endpoint.

Then we need to handle the response received from the HTTP driver, in this case the model will take care of it by preparing the data for the view:

```
const model = (actions$, HTTP) => {
    return HTTP.select(CATEGORY)
                    .flatten()
                    .map(parseResponse)
                    .map(simplifyData)
}
```

As we can see the model receives the actions stream and the HTTP object, and in this case we don't need to perform anything with the data inserted by the user because the response from the endpoint is providing all the data we need but potentially we could combine the data received and the user actions in order to prepare a new state for the view.

The last part is merging the data prepared from the model with the view and generating the virtual DOM elements that will be passed to the DOM driver:

```
const view = state$ => {
    return state$.map(generateVDOM)
                    .startWith(h1("Loading..."))
}
```

So our main function now will look like:

```
const main = sources => {
    const actions$ = intent(sources.DOM);
    const state$ = model(actions$, sources.HTTP)
    const vdom$ = view(state$);

    return {
        DOM: vdom$,
        HTTP: actions$
    }
}
```

Then we can take a look at the full example with MVI applied:

```
import xs from 'xstream';
import {run} from '@cycle/run';
import {makeDOMDriver, div, h1, h2, h3, img, p, input, button} from
'@cycle/dom';
import {makeHTTPDriver} from '@cycle/http';
import moment from 'moment';

const CATEGORY = "forecast";
const INIT_CITY = "London";

const getForm = () => div(".form", [
    input("#location-input"),
    button("#location-btn", "get forecasts")
])

const generateNext5Days = forecasts => {
    const list = forecasts.map(forecast => {
        return div(".forecast-box", [
            h3(moment(forecast.date).format("dddd Do MMM")),
            p(`min ${forecast.day.mintemp_c}°C - max ${forecast.day.
            maxtemp_c}°C`),
            img(".forecast-img", {
                props: {
                    src: `http:${forecast.day.condition.icon}`
                }
            }),
            p(".status", forecast.day.condition.text)
        ])
    });
    return div(".forecasts-container", list)
}

const generateCurrentForecast = forecast => div(".current-forecast-
container", [
    div(".today-forecast", [
            img(".forecast-img", {
```

```
                props: {
                    src: `http:${forecast.condition.icon}`
                }
            }),
            p(".status", forecast.condition.text)
        ]),
        h3(moment(forecast.last_updated).format("dddd Do MMMM YYYY")),
        h2(`${forecast.temp_c}°C`),
        p(`humidity: ${forecast.humidity}%`)
    ])

const generateVDOM = data => div(".main-container", [
        h1(`Your forecasts in ${data.city}`),
        getForm(),
        generateCurrentForecast(data.current),
        generateNext5Days(data.forecast)
    ])

const parseResponse = response => JSON.parse(response.text);
const simplifyData = data => {
                    return {
                        city: data.location.name,
                        current: data.current,
                        forecast: data.forecast.forecastday
                    }
                }

const getRequest = city => {
    return {
        url: `http://api.apixu.com/v1/forecast.json?key=04ca1fa2705645e4830
        214415172307&q=${city}&days=7`,
        category: CATEGORY
    }
}
```

```
const model = (actions$, HTTP) => {
    return HTTP.select(CATEGORY)
                .flatten()
                .map(parseResponse)
                .map(simplifyData)
}

const intent = DOM => {
    const input$ = DOM.select("#location-input").events("focusout")
                                .map(evt => evt.target.value);
    const btn$ = DOM.select("#location-btn").events("mousedown");
    return xs.combine(input$, btn$)
            .map(([city, mouseEvt])=> getRequest(city))
            .startWith(getRequest(INIT_CITY))
}

const view = state$ => {
    return state$.map(generateVDOM)
                .startWith(h1("Loading..."))
}

const main = sources => {
    const actions$ = intent(sources.DOM);
    const state$ = model(actions$, sources.HTTP)
    const vdom$ = view(state$);

    return {
        DOM: vdom$,
        HTTP: actions$
    }
}

const drivers = {
  DOM: makeDOMDriver('#app'),
  HTTP: makeHTTPDriver()
};

run(main, drivers);
```

MVI is not as complicated as it looks like; we just need to get used to it.

I'd like to highlight a few key concepts that we need to bear in mind when we integrate this architecture in a Cycle.js application:

- First of all, we transform our Cycle.js project to a structured project where each part can be reused and tested in isolation.

- This architecture allows us to even go further applying the MVI architecture to each single component: a MVI architecture applied to the form, one to the current day, and one for the list of the weekdays due to its nature.

- Communicating with streams allow the entire architecture to be more flexible and enhance the separation of concerns.

Before concluding the chapter with an overview of what Cycle.js brings to the reactive programming world, we need to enhance this example once again, introducing the official Cycle.js state management called Onionify.

Cycle.js and State Management

After seeing MVI in action, our journey continues with Onionify, a library created for managing the application state in Cycle.js.

As we know, handling the state is the key part of any web application. Cycle.js provides a unique approach to that, slightly different from what we are used to seeing with Angular or Redux.

Onionify is a tiny library (2kb only) with only one purpose: managing the application state in Cycle applications.

This library doesn't provide a driver, as we have seen in other occasions, but instead Onionify is wrapping the entire Cycle.js application with a unique state that is injected across multiple components.

The application state is a stream managed internally by Onionify, and each component can manipulate its own state and the parent components one via reducers.

The components need to be "isolated" with the homonymous library called **isolate**.

Isolate is a utility provided by Cycle.js that allows us to literally isolate a component, sharing only the sources provided by the main application; or a parent component, and returning a sink object that could be shared with the main application and/or other components.

Let's stop here for a moment and try to gather what we have learned until now about Cycle.js:

- We know that we can create an application with an MVI architecture.

- MVI could be applied not only to an entire Cycle application but could be applied to components too.

- This leads to the same architecture applied at all the levels of our architecture where sinks and sources are the only way to communicate between objects.

Considering all these facts, we can say that with Cycle.js, applying MVI, we can create a **Fractal architecture** that will allow us to use always the same "piece" (model view intent) for generating a bigger composition made by identical pieces applied several times.

Fractal architecture   Fractal architecture is not a new concept in the software development. This architecture with identical subsystems structures allows a high separation of concerns in order to shape a large project where modifying, deleting, or creating new parts won't affect the entire application considering the isolation in which the subsystems live.

Onionify applied in conjunction with MVI architecture helps by creating a solid and reusable architecture with strong separation of concerns and good encapsulation.

Therefore we should be able to reuse part of our Cycle.js application in others just respecting the contract our components need, so using the correct sources (drivers and streams) and interacting with the sinks returned by them.

In order to see Onionify in action, we are going to modify our weather application once again, splitting our MVI application in multiple components and using Onionify for changing the state.

Figure 4-5 shows what our Cycle.js application will look like after introducing Onionify.

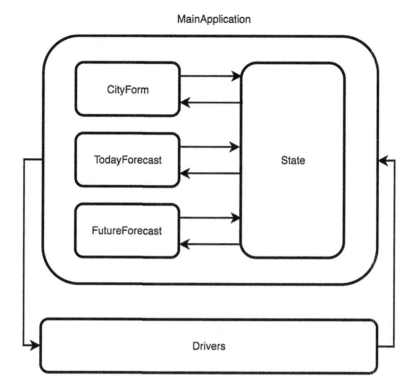

Figure 4-5. *Cycle Onionify project diagram*

Let's analyze what we have here compared to the previous application:

- We have three components: CityForm, TodayForecast, and FutureForecast.

- We have a state that is passed by our main application to the Onionify wrapper composed by the state observable.

- We still have the communication with drivers in the same way we worked before; therefore we still have the HTTP and DOM drivers.

CityForm is the component with the main logic, and it is responsible for retrieving what the user is typing inside the input field and also to prepare the request that will perform then by the HTTP driver.

```
import onionify from 'cycle-onionify';
import xs from 'xstream';
import {div, input, button, h1} from '@cycle/dom';

const INIT_CITY = "London";
const CITY_SEARCH = "citySearchAction";
const CATEGORY = "forecast";

const getRequest = city => ({
        type: CITY_SEARCH,
        city: city,
        url: `http://api.apixu.com/v1/forecast.json?key=04ca1fa2705645e4830
            214415172307&q=${city}&days=7`,
        category: CATEGORY
})

const getForm = location => div(".form", [
    h1(`Your forecasts in ${location.city}`),
    input("#location-input", {props: {value: `${location.city}`}}),
    button("#location-btn", "get forecasts")
])

const parseResponse = response => JSON.parse(response.text);
const simplifyData = data => function changeState(prevState) {
                        return {
                            city: data.location.name,
                            current: data.current,
                            forecasts: data.forecast.forecastday
                        }
                    }

const model = (actions$, HTTP) => {
    const reducer$ = HTTP.select(CATEGORY)
                .flatten()
                .map(parseResponse)
                .map(simplifyData)

    return reducer$
}
```

```
const intent = DOM => {
    const input$ = DOM.select("#location-input").events("focusout")
                        .map(evt => evt.target.value);
    const btn$ = DOM.select("#location-btn").events("mousedown");

    return xs.combine(input$, btn$)
            .map(([city, mouseEvt]) => getRequest(city))
            .startWith(getRequest(INIT_CITY))

}

const view = state$ => state$.map(state => getForm(state))

export const CityForm = sources => {
    const state$ = sources.onion.state$;
    const actions$ = intent(sources.DOM);
    const reducer$ = model(actions$, sources.HTTP);
    const vdom$ = view(state$);

    return {
        DOM: vdom$,
        onion: reducer$,
        HTTP: actions$
    }
}
```

As we can immediately recognize, we have a new parameter from the sources that is provided by Onionify wrapper; this library provides an onion object that contains the state stream, based on that we can interact with the parent state stream, reacting to that, or manipulating the internal component state as well.

Overall the component is very similar to what we had in the previous application, and the only change is related to the application state that represents the response coming from the weather API, so the CityForm is using the state stream just for retrieving the location chosen by the user.

The last thing to mention is to understand what this component is returning as sink and how we can immediately spot the onion property containing the HTTP response as the state of the application.

As we can recognize, this component is self-contained, so if we would like to reuse it in another application we would be able to do it without the need for changing anything: that's the power of working with a fractal architecture where the reusability, separation of concerns, and encapsulation are first citizens in the architecture.

Before investigating how we need to modify App.js for handling Onionify library, let's do a quick tour of the other two passive components: TodayForecast and FutureForecast.

These two components are passive because they just need to render some content provided by the state; they don't have user interactions and they are not going to manipulate any parent state or perform new HTTP requests.

This is the TodayForecast component:

```
import {div, h2, h3, img, p} from '@cycle/dom';
import moment from 'moment';

const generateCurrentForecast = forecast => div(".current-forecast-
container", [
    div(".today-forecast", [
            img(".forecast-img", {
            props: {
                src: `http:${forecast.condition.icon}`
            }
        }),
        p(".status", forecast.condition.text)
    ]),
    h3(moment(forecast.last_updated).format("dddd Do MMMM YYYY")),
    h2(`${forecast.temp_c}°C`),
    p(`humidity: ${forecast.humidity}%`)
])

const view = state$ => state$.map(state => generateCurrentForecast(state.
current))

export const TodayForecast = sources => {
    const state$ = sources.onion.state$;
    const vdom$ = view(state$)
```

```
    return {
        DOM: vdom$
    }
}
```

In this chunk of code we can spot in the TodayForecast function the state stream for rendering the view that corresponds to the weather data representation for the specific moment when the user is requesting the forecasts.

Considering this is a passive component, its only duty is providing the virtual dom to the DOM driver for rendering the view.

Obviously, in case of any user interaction that could change the application state, this will be reflected in the sink and it would have been able to share the new state via the onionify property of our sink – the same in case it would need to trigger a new HTTP request to the weather forecast endpoint.

Let's take a look to the FutureForecast component then:

```javascript
import {div, h3, img, p} from '@cycle/dom';
import moment from 'moment';

const generateNext5Days = forecasts => {
    const list = forecasts.map(forecast => div(".forecast-box", [
            h3(moment(forecast.date).format("dddd Do MMM")),
            p(`min ${forecast.day.mintemp_c}°C - max ${forecast.day.
            maxtemp_c}°C`),
            img(".forecast-img", {
                props: {
                    src: `http:${forecast.day.condition.icon}`
                }
            }),
            p(".status", forecast.day.condition.text)
        ])
    );

    return div(".forecasts-container", list)
}

const view = state$ => state$.map(state => generateNext5Days(state.
forecasts))
```

```
export const FutureForecast = sources => {
    const state$ = sources.onion.state$;
    const vdom$ = view(state$)

    return {
        DOM: vdom$
    }
}
```

Also, this component is very similar to the previous one, and it doesn't need to share any state update. It's just consuming the state stream in order to render the new virtual dom to provide to the DOM driver.

Finally, it's the turn of App.js where we can find the glue for our "onionified application":

```
import xs from 'xstream';
import {run} from '@cycle/run';
import {makeDOMDriver, div, h1} from '@cycle/dom';
import {makeHTTPDriver} from '@cycle/http';
import isolate from '@cycle/isolate';
import onionify from 'cycle-onionify';
import {CityForm} from './CityForm';
import {TodayForecast} from './TodayForecast';
import {FutureForecast} from './FutureForecast';

const generateVDOM = ([formVNode, todayVNode, futureVNode]) => div(".main-
container", [
        formVNode,
        todayVNode,
        futureVNode
    ])
const view = (locationDOM$, todayForecastDOM$, futureForecastDOM$) => {
    return xs.combine(locationDOM$, todayForecastDOM$, futureForecastDOM$)
            .map(combinedStreams => generateVDOM(combinedStreams))
            .startWith(h1("Loading..."));
}
```

```
const main = sources => {
    const cityLens = {
        get: state => state,
        set: (state, childState) => childState
    }

    const locationSink = isolate(CityForm, {onion: cityLens})(sources);
    const todayForecastSink = isolate(TodayForecast, {onion: cityLens})
    (sources);
    const futureForecastSink = isolate(FutureForecast, {onion: cityLens})
    (sources);

    const locationReducer$ = locationSink.onion;
    const httpRequest$ = locationSink.HTTP;

    const vdom$ = view(locationSink.DOM,
                       todayForecastSink.DOM,
                       futureForecastSink.DOM);
    return {
        DOM: vdom$,
        HTTP: httpRequest$,
        onion: locationReducer$
    }
}

const drivers = {
  DOM: makeDOMDriver('#app'),
  HTTP: makeHTTPDriver()
};

const mainOnionified = onionify(main);

run(mainOnionified, drivers);
```

Here we can find quite a few interesting new concepts, so let's start to describe what we are doing from the end of our JavaScript file.

As we mentioned, Onionify is not a driver but a wrapper around our application; therefore we used it for wrapping our main function and we passed the decorated, or onionified, version of our main function to the run method.

This allows us to pass the state through different components via the onionify property in our sources and sinks.

Let's now take a look on what the main function looks like. We start with a lens called cityLens. Lenses are used when a component needs to access the same object of its parent like in our case but also when we need to manipulate the state before it lands into a specific component.

Technically speaking a lens is an object with a getter and a setter, nothing really complicated, but they are very useful in functional programming specifically when we use them for composing objects. Lenses are also well known in the Haskell language, in the JavaScript world they are used in conjunction with Immutable.js, and definitely they are present in Ramda (lensProp method for instance), a JavaScript functional library.

After the lens definition, which will allow us to share the data present in the component with the others, we have the instantiation of our three custom components with the isolate utility offered by Cycle.js.

We are passing the lens to each component and the sources, and this allows us to get interaction with the parent component inside each component. In this case it's the parent component in the application itself but it's clear by the approach, working in this way, we can wrap our component defining a standard input/output contract and reuse it easily in different parts of the same application or even better in other applications.

After creating the instances of our components it's time to pass the manipulated state and the HTTP request to the associated properties in our sink object.

In this case we need to highlight a couple of things. In this project the state is handled by the endpoint response, and there isn't any manipulation from other components that are just used for the rendering phase.

Obviously, if we check other examples present in the Onionify repository (http://bit.ly/2eQXh9S), we can see that instead of passing just a stream as an application state like we are doing, we can combine multiple streams from different components in order to store a more complex application state.

The last bit is retrieving all the streams containing the virtual dom prepared by the different components and combine them all together for producing the look and feel of our Cycle application.

For doing that, we create a view method that collects all the streams and combines them in a unique one that will generate the final stream with the virtual dom that will be rendered by the DOM driver.

I'd like to get your attention on the way we are doing that because as you can see, it's a little bit verbose, in particular when the application grows and we need to merge multiple components.

In these cases we should prepare some utils methods for handling these situations (wrapping in a single or multiple functions would make the deal). Cycle.js doesn't come with anything useful out of the box, but there are some libraries that are aiming for that. At the moment, however, there is nothing official for achieving a more readable and flexible approach.

Wrap-Up

In this chapter, we evaluated our first fully reactive framework, understanding what Cycle.js brings to the table, and the different architectural approaches used for achieving that.

Cycle is maintained by a small but very talented community that is porting many reactive and functional concepts from other languages in the JavaScript community.

I believe that it is one of the most innovative approaches we can find in the front-end reactive architecture ecosystem at the moment. MVI is, in my opinion, merging the best from older architectures like MVP, for instance, and the unidirectional flow that is characterizing the latest front-end architectures like Redux.

There is still a lot to do in our reactive journey, so it's time to move on and talk about our next functional reactive state management library: MobX.

CHAPTER 5

MobX: Simple State Management

Do, or do not. There is no 'try.'

—Yoda

After a deep dive into the first reactive framework, we can continue our journey discovering others' reactive architectures, reviewing a flexible and easy-to-use state management system like MobX.

MobX is simple but very effective state management system that we can integrate in many projects independently from the stack we are using.

Obviously being simple doesn't mean incomplete; we can really structure complex applications with the help of MobX state tree: an opinionated, transactional and MobX powered state container heavily based on the tree data structure for handling the application state.

During this chapter, we are going to review a couple of examples that will give us an idea of how to structure a MobX application and what are the benefits of using it in our projects.

Introduction to MobX

The philosophy behind MobX is very simple:

Anything that can be derived from the application state, should be derived. Automatically.

© Luca Mezzalira 2018
L. Mezzalira, *Front-End Reactive Architectures*, https://doi.org/10.1007/978-1-4842-3180-7_5

Usually when we have a non-reactive application and we want to update its state, we create methods for manipulating manually specific parts of the model and for updating the views, potentially causing inconsistency between the two, sometimes increasing the coupling between them.

With MobX we are trying to minimize these situations having an automated update, via subscription (**observer**), to reactions that happened at the application state level (**observables**).

MobX has a few key concepts to remember in order to properly embrace the library:

- **Observables** are used to derive the state of our application; the rule of thumb here is that an observable should store a value that defines a state in our applications.

- **Computed Values** are properties used for deriving automatically complex values from the application state using functions in a synchronous manner; this mechanism allows better predictability and debugging of our computed values. Computed values are updated lazily.

- **Reactions** are similar to computed values because are generating new values starting from the application state but in this case they are used for generating side effects.

- **Actions** are the method used for changing the application state; if we specify to use MobX in strict mode, actions are the only way for updating our application state.

- **Observers** are used in the views for reacting to any state change.

With just these concepts we can start to build a simple MobX application to get familiar with it.

MobX finds the perfect fit with Virtual DOM libraries like React.js; actually, React and MobX are a great combination for creating reactive applications, but obviously this won't mean other frameworks are out of scope, but React is combined perfectly with the MobX philosophy.

Before going ahead, let's see MobX in practice with a simple counter:

```
import React from 'react';
import ReactDOM from 'react-dom';
import {observable} from 'mobx';
import {observer} from 'mobx-react';
```

```
const counterState = observable({
    value: 0,
    inc: function(){
        counter.value++
    },
    dec: function(){
        counter.value--
    }
});

@observer
export class Counter extends React.Component{
    render(){
        return (<div>
            {this.props.state.value}
            <div>
                <button type="button" onClick={this.props.state.inc}>
                increment</button>
                <button type="button" onClick={this.props.state.dec}>
                decrement</button>
            </div>
        </div>)
    }
}

ReactDOM.render(
    <Counter state={counterState}></Counter>,
    document.getElementById("app")
);
```

In this example, we used React.js creating a component called Counter and passing an external object called counterState that represents the application state.

CounterState is an observable, and it contains a property called value that is updated by two actions (inc and dec functions). The observable object, created in this way, automatically treats the methods that are updating the observable as actions.

Every time one of these actions is triggered by the user interface, the value property will be updated and, by reaction, the view that is observing the application state.

If we now check the React component we can immediately spot an @observer – this is a decorator that wraps our component into a function allowing us to create the reaction between what is observed in the React component and the application state present in the MobX observable.

ES7 DECORATORS AND MOBX PROJECT SETUP

The Decorator pattern is used to express high-order function with a simple syntax; in fact, a decorator expressed with the syntax @decoratorName, it represents a function that is wrapping another function, extending its behavior.

Decorators in JavaScript are introduced with ES7; therefore they are a fairly new addition to JavaScript specifications, and any decorator we are using in our examples can be removed if you prefer working directly with functions, as they are just a convenient way that MobX provides them out of the box to save you from having to write tons of code.

In our example, we were decorating a React component in order to augment its behaviors and observe any change happening to a computed value or an observable.

When we work with decorators and we use transpilers like Babel, we need to remember to set up the MobX project correctly using the Babel's plug-ins: *babel-plugin-transform-decorators-legacy* and *babel-plugintransform-decorators*.

These two plug-ins allow our MobX project to be transpiled correctly without any issue. Anyway, you can consult the setup of our examples, as they are all using Babel in combination with webpack and I kept to the bare minimum modules to strictly transpile the project.

In few lines of code we were able to create a simple MobX – React application separating completely the application state and its behaviors from the user interface, allowing us to potentially reuse these two elements or changing them without incurring any potential bugs introduced by the changes.

Also, MobX embraces fully the reactive paradigm where the application state is updated via observables decoupling de facto the view from the model via a common contract that can be understood by the two main actors.

A nice thing to highlight is how MobX optimizes the computed values updated behind the scenes; this reactive library is taking care of updating only the computed values that are linked to a specific state, only when they change, and it won't compute all the others present in the application.

The mechanism is very similar to what React.js is doing during the reconciliation phase: checking what are the differences inside the dependency tree and via a diffing algorithm, updating only the values that should be changed, maintaining high performances also when the tree is deep and complex like in large applications.

REACT RECONCILIATION AND MOBX DIFFING ALGORITHM

React and MobX are sharing a couple of concepts like the diffing algorithm. Understanding how these algorithms work is very important because we can improve the performance of our applications just by following the best practices described in the documentation. Therefore I thought it would be beneficial to share some links for getting deeper into this argument:

React reconciliation: `http://bit.ly/2xHYifx`

In-depth explanation of MobX: `http://bit.ly/2g2fYIW`

Fundamental principles behind MobX: `http://bit.ly/2x7YcJL`

After this introduction on the key elements behind MobX, it's time to see a MobX application in the real world, so in this case we are going to build a MobX and React application based on an image gallery and the same one with MobX state tree. In this way we can compare the two approaches, understanding the pros and cons of both and describing the different architectural approach.

Our First Application with MobX and React

In this chapter's projects, we are exploring four key architectural areas to cover in the majority of front-end applications like these:

- How the data flow is managed inside an application.

- How to handle user interactions.

- How to consume remote endpoints.

- How to manage the application's state.

The application we are going to build is an image gallery similar to Figure 5-1.

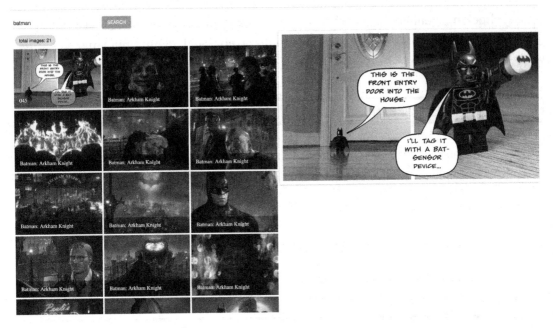

Figure 5-1. *The project UI*

It could be interpreted as a component of a larger application but it's important to cover the concepts listed above and then we will be able to replicate them in projects at scale.

The service we are going to consume for searching images is the Flickr APIs. Flickrs allow us to perform a search on their catalogue based on a specific search term.

Figure 5-2 shows how our MobX application is structured.

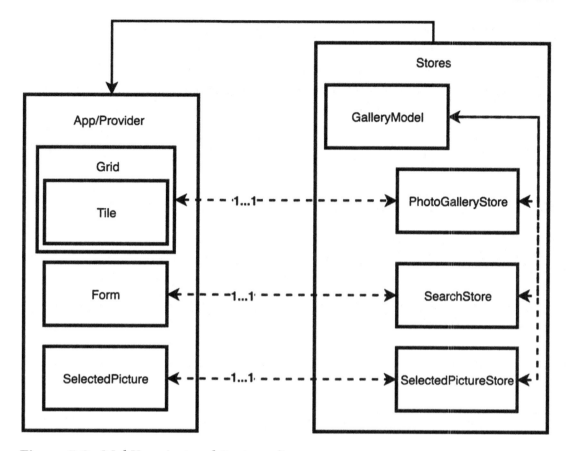

Figure 5-2. *MobX project architecture diagram*

On the left of the diagram we have all the views, and in our case are passive views that are used only for rendering the user interface and gathering the interactions handled by the stores.

Each view has a 1 to 1 relation with a store; this is very similar to what we have done in the second chapter when we analyzed the MVP architecture.

Doing it will guarantee a great separation of concerns (view representation and application behaviours are separated) and components reusability (we could change completely the views without affecting the application behaviours and vice-versa) – two important principles to take into consideration in any software architecture.

On the right we have instead all the stores instantiated from the stores object. In each store we are going to inject an application model called GalleryModel.

This is not a concept requested by MobX, but we want to create solid architectures with great flexibility and high code standards, creating a model that will allow us to gather all the application states, or component states, inside a unique object that will be visible to all the stores.

In this way, it will be easier to maintain separation of the different stores that are not aware of the existence of others and on top will facilitate the application debugging because the application state is present in a unique place instead of being spread in different stores.

Considering MobX uses observables for storing the application state, this means that inside the model we are going to have observables and potentially some actions for changing the observable, but all the computed values will be closer to the view at the store level.

Let's now take a look at the folder structure used for this project.

Examining the Folder Structure

Obviously, the project is also available on the Github repository of this book, so feel free to download it to better help you to follow the next steps.

As you can see in Figure 5-3 the folder structure resembles our architecture with a separation per file type (stores, models, components. and so on) instead of a domain approach (a search folder, am image gallery folder...).

Figure 5-3. *MobX project structure*

In large applications I usually prefer gathering the files in domain folders, and this could really help to understand better the application, in particular, for new developers that are approaching the application for the first time. This way it's easier to find a correlation of what we see on the screen and the folder name when the names are meaningful enough.

It is time to write our MobX application, but the first thing we do is to compose the general structure of our application, defining it in the App.js file. We need to create three main React components: a text input for performing a search, a pictures grid, and a selected image component for better viewing an image.

```
...
@observer
export class App extends React.Component{
    render(){
        return (
        <Provider {...stores}>
            <MuiThemeProvider>
                <div>
                    <Form/>
                    <Grid style={style.child}/>
                    <SelectedPicture style={style.child}/>
                </div>
            </MuiThemeProvider>
        </Provider>)
    }
}

ReactDOM.render(
    <App/>,
    document.getElementById("app")
);
```

There are a couple of things to highlight in these few lines of code: first of all is the observer decorator. We have already seen it in the first MobX example; the decorator allows us to react to a state change triggering the render function inside the React component like it would happen when we change the props or state property.

Another key thing of the component is called Provider, wrapping our entire UI. This is provided by MobX-React library and it's a utility for specifying a context that will be accessible by any part of the application.

In this case, MobX is using it for providing access to the store objects inside any of our components via a dependency injection mechanism that we are going to see in action when we discuss stores.

The Provider object contains a property called stores where we are providing all the stores that compose this application:

```
...
const model = new Model();
const photoGallery = new PhotoGalleryStore(model);
const search = new SearchStore(model);
const selectedPicture = new SelectedPictureStore(model);

export {
    photoGallery,
    search,
    selectedPicture
}
```

In the stores object, we just exposed the three stores that interact with the views they are linked to.

As we have seen before in the project architecture diagram, we want to have a 1 to 1 correlation between views and stores; this will help us in the future by reusing a specific part of a MobX application in other projects.

An important thing to describe is the role of the Model object, in the tradition of MobX architecture we don't have the concept of a model where the application state is spread across multiple stores.

In our application instead, we used that for wrapping all the observables that represent the application state, leaving the domain-specific observables, the computed values, and the actions inside the stores.

We are using this technique because otherwise, in order to change the value or observe a specific observable present in another store, we would need to get access and knowledge to other stores not only exposing the observable but potentially having the possibility to call actions or other methods available in the store itself.

In this way, we have the application state represented inside the model that is injected inside each store, and they can observe or change the application state directly. This, in conjunction with the reactive paradigm, will trigger to update all the computed values that are observing a specific observable and it will update the related views.

The search domain is composed by an input text with a button:

```
...
@inject('search')
@observer
export default class Form extends React.Component{
    setSearchTerm(evt){
        this.props.search.changeSearchTerm(evt.target.value)
    }

    search(){
        this.props.search.requestPics();
    }

    getButton(){
        return (
            <RaisedButton label="SEARCH" primary={true} style={style}
            onClick={this.search.bind(this)}/>
        )
    }

    getSpinner(){
        return (
            <CircularProgress size={35} thickness={5}/>
        )
    }

    render(){
        return (
            <div>
                <TextField hintText="e.g. Bear" onBlur={this.setSearchTerm.
                bind(this)}/>
                {
                    this.props.search.isSearching ? this.getSpinner() :
                    this.getButton()
                }
```

```
        </div>
    )
  }
}
```

In the React components we can also inject our stores in order to interact with them; the rule of thumb here is always decoupling the behavior of our components from the look and feel; delegating, de facto, their logic to the store that will be responsible to interact with the rest of the application; retrieving from a remote endpoint; or manipulating the application state.

This approach allows us to change the views without introducing bugs in their behaviors and also it definitely helps in the testing of the components and their behaviors because it becomes very easy to define the boundaries of the two worlds.

MobX provides an inject decorator for implementing the dependency injection; therefore we can use this decorator for injecting the store inside the React component.

The store is accessible via the props property available in any React component, so we can call a method simply writing *this.props.store.method* where store is the name we assigned to the store and method is the name of the method we want to call.

The last important highlight of this component is the variable isSearching, clearly a Boolean, which is an observable with a domain specific to this component and not to the entire application. This property won't be shared across other stores, so we can define it in the store dedicated to the Form component instead of defining it as an application state.

As an observable, every time the value changes, the view subscribed to the observable property will automatically react to the change, calling the render function again.

Let's see how the Form's store is implemented:

```
import {observable, computed, action} from 'mobx';
import Config from '../configs/Configuration';

export default class SearchStore{
    @observable isSearching = false;

    constructor(model){
        this.model = model;
    }
```

```
@computed get url(){
    return Config.getSearchURL(this.model.searchTerm);
}

@action changeSearchTerm(term){
    this.model.searchTerm = term;
}

@action requestPics(){
    this.isSearching = true;
    fetch(this.url)
        .then(this.onData)
        .then(this.onResult.bind(this))
}

@action onData(response){
    return response.json();
}

@action onResult(response){
    this.isSearching = false;
    this.model.picsList = response.photos.photo.map(value => {
        return {
            id: value.id,
            title: value.title,
            image: Config.getPicURL(value),
            large_image: Config.getLargePicURL(value)
        }
    });
}
}
```

In the constructor, we have the model injected when we instantiated the store, and we have also the isSearching property as an observable like we described before.

Finally we see in practice the computed values and the actions mentioned at the beginning of this chapter.

In this store, we have a getter for the URL used for searching the images on Flickr, and this computed value will return a new URL every time the searchTerm changes (observable present in the model). We are going to review the main model at the end of this description.

I'd like to capture your attention on the Config object; this is used as a static object for composing the URLs inside the application and in this case, we are just importing the Config object in the store that needs it, but in the next example on the MobX state tree, we are going to see a different approach that is way more elegant.

Every time the textinput triggers the blur event we are calling the changeSearchTerm method in the store, updating the observable in the model.

Instead, once the user is clicking the search button in the UI, we are performing the search method (*requestPics* method), and there we immediately change the isSearching observable forcing the component to update substituting the button with a spinner preventing the possibility of additional requests to the server.

After that we are performing the real request to the Flickr APIs layer and once we retrieve the response, we are storing in the application model a filtered version of the data we received, composing also the URLs for the small and big pictures (*onResult* method).

As we have seen until now, we have updated few observables that represent the application state, inside the model object; now it's time to see what the model looks like:

```
import {autorun, observable} from 'mobx'

export default class GalleryModel{
    @observable searchTerm = "";
    @observable picsList = [];
    @observable selectedPictureURL = null;

    constructor(){
        autorun(()=> {
            if(this.picsList.length > 0){
                this.selectedPictureURL = this.picsList[0].large_image
            }
        })
    }
}
```

Our model is composed of a bunch of observables that can be available to all the stores; therefore any computed values that are using them will react to the change.

Also in the constructor we can see another MobX method, autorun, which is used for handling side effects, in our case every time we are changing the picsList array we are defining the first image selected so the user will be able to see an image without interacting with the grid.

In this case we wouldn't be able to use computed values because they can be only getter related to a specific observable value; so *autorun* comes to the rescue by observing any value expressed in its body and reacting every time this value is updated.

Autorun, like computed values, is reacting only when a change happens to an observable. It's very handy in situations like this one where we need to create a side effect because the alternative would have been to change the *selectedPictureURL* inside a store that shouldn't be aware of the existence of this value, considering it's not using it all.

Instead, with autorun we can wrap the update logic inside the model maintaining the contract where each store is related 1 to 1 with its view and update the application state related to itself without being aware of the existence of other observable.

In the SearchStore we update the value of the picsList observable inside the main model. Now it's the turn of the grid component that will render the results retrieved from the remote service.

```
...
@inject('photoGallery')
@observer
export default class Grid extends React.Component{
    render(){
        const tiles = this.props.photoGallery.pics.map(pic => {
            return (
                <Tile key={pic.id} data={pic}/>
            )
        })

        return (
          <div style={styles.root}>
            <Chip style={styles.chip}>
                {`total images: ${this.props.photoGallery.totalPics}`}
            </Chip>
```

```
        <GridList
            cellHeight={180}
            cols={3}
            padding={5}
            style={styles.gridList}>
                {tiles}
        </GridList>
      </div>
    )
  }
}
```

The Grid component has its own store, `photoGallery`, and it's retrieving from there two main values: the pictures array and a property called `totalPics` used for displaying how many pictures were retrieved from the service.

Another thing to notice is that we are dynamically creating the `Tile` components for populating the `GridList` component, and the tiles are created anytime we are updating the `pics` property from the store.

The store for the grid component is this one:

```
import {observable, computed, action, autorun} from 'mobx'

export default class PhotoGalleryStore {
    constructor(model){
        this.model = model;
    }

    @computed get pics(){
        return this.model.picsList
    }

    @computed get totalPics(){
        return this.model.picsList.length;
    }

    @action selectedPicture(url){
        this.model.selectedPictureURL = url;
    }
}
```

As we can immediately spot, the pics property is a computed value. This is a suggestion I provide because if, for any given reason, we need to change the model or the store, we won't have any coupling with the view, as long the contract between the objects remains the same then we would be able to refactor what we need without affecting the view.

Also, the model is totally decoupled from the view, like in the MVP architecture, embracing, in a simple way, future changes inside our application and making it more robust and easy to test.

Every time the user is clicking on a picture we need to change the image selected, but in order to do that we need to see who is calling the selectedPicture method present in the PhotoGalleryStore.

```
...
@inject('photoGallery')
@observer
export default class Tile extends React.Component{
    selectedPic(e){
        this.props.photoGallery.selectedPicture(this.props.data.large_image)
    }

    render(){
        return (
            <GridTile
                style={styles.gridTile}
                onClick={this.selectedPic.bind(this)}
                title={this.props.data.title}>
                <img src={this.props.data.image} />
            </GridTile>
        )
    }
}
```

In the Tile component, we are injecting the photoGallery store instance; this gives us the possibility of changing the large image by simply providing the large image URL present in the props object of the single tile.

The selectedPicture method will then update the observable in the model where we store the picture URL to use for retrieving the large image, so the last bit of this example is introducing the SelectedPicture component.

```
...
@inject('selectedPicture')
@observer
export default class SelectedPicture extends React.Component{
    render(){
        const url = this.props.selectedPicture.picPath;

        return (
            <Card style={style}>
                <CardMedia>
                    {
                        url ? <img src={url} /> : ""
                    }
                </CardMedia>
            </Card>
        )
    }
}
```

This component is really simple; we are just displaying a different image every time the url property changes. Here also here we can see the MobX pattern for injecting a store (selectedPicture store) and to observe any change happening to a computed value or observable.

The store for the SelectedPicture component is composed in this way:

```
import {computed, action} from 'mobx';

export default class SelectedPictureStore{
    constructor(model){
        this.model = model;
    }

    @computed get picPath(){
        return this.model.selectedPictureURL || ""
    }
}
```

Also in this case we are not providing the observable to the view but just a computed value via a getter.

Figure 5-4 shows the data flow in this application.

1. The user interacts with the UI that calls an action in the store.

2. The action updates an observable in the main model.

3. All the computed values subscribed to that observable are updating the value.

4. The computed values or observables present in the views are causing the render of the component with the new state.

Figure 5-4. *Data flow diagram*

This is a simple MobX example that provides the idea of how this framework is using the reactive programming paradigm via observables.

As we can see, the single responsibility principle is respected and in a certain way enforced by the observables, computed values, and actions.

At the same time we can spot a certain freedom that probably won't help much in larger teams where any developer could possibly interpret this flexibility as a way to take shortcuts if needed.

Not only for this reason but also for providing a more structured way for writing large applications, we can possibly use MobX state tree, an opinionated library that is creating clear boundaries around the application structure, and it helps to create a solid and scalable architecture enforcing the concepts of automatic derivation and immutable state in an effective way.

MobX State Tree

As the name suggests, MobX state tree is based on immutable trees, in particular the benefits provided by this library are the following:

- The possibility to write "imperative" code that hides a reactive implementation, so the learning curve for new developers approaching the reactive paradigm should be easier.

- Mutable data structure where behind the scenes an immutable tree snapshot is created and maintained by the library itself, providing also the possibility to work very well with isomorphic applications where we can inject the tree for a specific state and the application would react to that.

- Store type system available out of the box with the possibility to specify primitive and custom values.

- Life-cycle hooks at the store level, similar to the ones we can find in a React component.

- Clear boundaries on how to structure the stores and how to update the application states.

These are just a few of the key features provided by MobX state tree.

The interesting point of MobX state tree is the fact we are dealing with a tree structure, similar to what we are used to when we work with the DOM on the UI.

At the same time, this means we have a strong hierarchy to deal with. Therefore when we structure our state trees we need to pay more attention to how we encapsulate our data and how we handle the dependencies between different branches of the tree.

The best way to understand the problems we might encounter using MobX state tree is trying to implement it in our previous project in order to find possible solutions and new approaches.

Refactoring the previous project won't require many changes; in fact the views will remain almost the same. Refer to Figure 5-5 for an eagle eye view of our architecture before deep diving inside the code.

Comparing this architecture with the previous one we immediately notice a few differences:

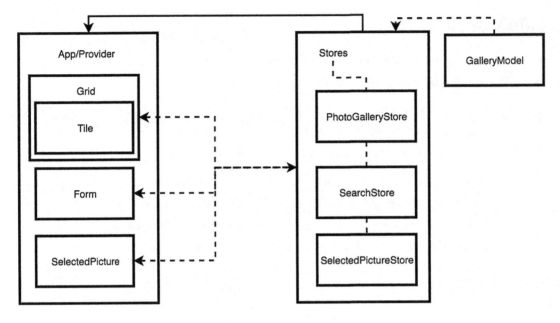

Figure 5-5. *MobX state tree application architecture*

- Inside the components we are going to inject the entire tree and not just a specific store like in the previous implementation.

- The GalleryModel is an object not created inside the stores but it's *composed* with the application tree.

- There is a hierarchy between stores with a root and multiple nodes (PhotoGalleryStore, SearchStore and SelectedPictureStore) so we could traverse bidirectionally the data across stores.

In a certain way, this last feature could be the most dangerous to deal with, because if we are not able to structure the stores in a smart way respecting our domain, we could end up in a large application with a lot of dependencies between stores, thus introducing coupling where it is not needed and complicating the evolution of our project or the refactor of specific design implementations.

A suggestion I feel that is useful to share is that we should structure our large applications with multiple trees, as this will help us to maintain and potentially reuse our code in a better way. The trick is always dividing by domain our application; when we are able to identify clearly the boundaries of a specific domain, structuring a state tree becomes easier.

After this brief excursus of MobX state tree architecture, it is time to see how we could apply this to our image gallery project, so we are going to analyze the differences compared with the previous project where we used just MobX with a custom architecture.

App.js introduces a few new concepts strictly related to the MobX state tree library:

```
...
const augmentedStore = types.compose(GalleryModel, Stores);
const PicsGalleryStore = augmentedStore.create({
    picsList: [],
    searchTerm: "",
    selectedPictureURL: ""
}, {config: Config});

@observer
export class App extends React.Component{
    render(){
        return (
            <Provider store={PicsGalleryStore}>
                <MuiThemeProvider>
                    <div>
                        <Form/>
                        <Grid style={style.child}/>
                        <SelectedPicture style={style.child}/>
                    </div>
                </MuiThemeProvider>
            </Provider>)
    }
}


ReactDOM.render(
```

```
  <App/>,
  document.getElementById("app")
)
```

The application structure remains the same, but before defining the component we are using the types object provided by the MobX state tree for composing the main application model with the different stores. This will allow us to access the application state present inside the model from the root of our application tree without the need to create additional nested nodes.

MobX state tree provides the possibility of composing trees and that is a very interesting feature mainly because our application could become quite large during the time, and working with composition over inheritance will allow us to be flexible enough for refactoring, adding new features, or making drastic changes without many problems.

Another thing to highlight is that inside our composed tree variable we are defining the initial values of the application state.

This is another feature of MobX state tree: it forces us to set a default value for mandatory objects like in this case the searchTerm, picsList, and the selectedPictureURL.

This feature is part of the checks that the MobX state tree is doing at runtime; without defining these values, the application will trigger a meaningful error regarding the root cause of the problem, thanks to the type system check present inside the library.

Finally, once we create the augmentedStore node, passing a third parameter for the configuration object, that is the way MobX state tree injects an object into a store; it's just a simple dependency injection mechanism.

This mechanism is very handy because it gives us the flexibility to inject multiple objects in a tree without the need to maintain singletons or instantiating different objects.

In this case we are using the dependency injection for the configuration utils but potentially we could use it for a logger object or any other utility that we want to use in our application.

The changes we have just seen in the main application lead to changes on the stores object:

```
import { types } from "mobx-state-tree"
import PhotoGalleryStore from './PhotoGalleryStore';
import SearchStore from './SearchStore';
import SelectedPictureStore from './SelectedPictureStore';
```

```
const stores = types.model({
    photoGallery: types.optional(PhotoGalleryStore, {}),
    search:types.optional(SearchStore, {}),
    selectedPicture: types.optional(SelectedPictureStore, {})
})
```

```
export default stores;
```

What we are doing is describing a tree composed by multiple nodes where we described the stores as optional values, appending them to the root of our state tree.

Types.model represents the shape of an object and we are going to see in the other stores how we have modified them in order to accommodate the key parts of MobX described in the previous section.

Considering the React components are maintaining the same structure from the previous examples, we are going to focus our attention on how MobX state tree handles stores and our custom addition of the model. We start with the GalleryModel:

```
import {types} from 'mobx-state-tree';
```

```
const Picture = types.model("Picture", {
    id: types.identifier(),
    title: types.string,
    image: types.string,
    large_image: types.string
})
```

```
const model = types.model({
    searchTerm: types.string,
    picsList: types.array(Picture),
    selectedPictureURL: types.string
}).actions(self => ({
    setPicsList(arr){
        self.picsList = arr;
    },
    setSelectedPictureURL(url){
        self.selectedPictureURL = url;
    },
    setSearchTerm(value){
```

```
        self.searchTerm = value;
    }
}))
```

```
export default model;
```

In this object we can start to see a more complete structure of a tree's node. In this case we have defined the state of our application that will guarantee reactions every time a value in the model changes: the first object right after the `types.model` definition represents the observables objects like we had in the previous MobX example.

Each of them need to be typed with a specific primitive or complex type like in the case of the `picsList` where we defined the Picture model that represents the data structure contained in each single element of our array.

This feature will save us a lot of debugging time because we are sure we cannot have data discrepancies inside our models. This is exactly what we expect: otherwise the application won't work.

This is also another reason why at the beginning I was suggesting that you invest time defining the application's domains; doing that will save you from the possibility of structuring your models in an incorrect way, producing de facto a system that will help out to resolve issues inside an application.

Therefore we should always start our projects defining our models and their interaction with the main tree and then focusing on the UI of our application.

Another constrain of MobX state tree is that we cannot update the observables directly but only via actions. These boundaries help a lot in large applications because they are providing direction without the possibility of having different implementations for achieving the same result. Therefore we have defined multiple actions for providing the possibility of updating the application state.

Inside the actions object implementation we have added the argument `self`: it's defined by the MobX for allowing us to maintain the right scope without creating a manual binding. `Self` will be available when we declare computed values later on in the chapter.

Now we can add another piece to our knowledge of our MobX state tree, introducing the computed values in a model like we have done in the `SearchStore`:

```
import { types, getParent, getEnv} from "mobx-state-tree";

const searchStore = types.model({
    isSearching: false,
```

```
    }).views(self => ({
        get url(){
            return getEnv(self).config.getSearchURL(getParent(self).searchTerm);
        }
    })).actions(self => ({
        requestPics(){
            self.isSearching = true;
            fetch(self.url)
                .then(self.onData)
                .then(self.onResult.bind(this))
                .catch((err) => console.log(err))
        },
        onData(response){
            return response.json();
        },
        onResult(response){
            const configuration = getEnv(self).config;
            const model = getParent(self);

            self.isSearching = false;
            const picsArr = response.photos.photo.map(value => {
                return {
                    id: value.id,
                    title: value.title,
                    image: configuration.getPicURL(value),
                    large_image: configuration.getLargePicURL(value)
                }
            })

            model.setPicsList(picsArr);
            model.setSelectedPictureURL(picsArr[0].large_image);
        },
        changeSearchTerm(term){
            getParent(self).setSearchTerm(term);
        },
    }))

export default searchStore;
```

In this case we added another element to our model called views, and the views are expressed with an object literal and they are the translation of computed values in a MobX state tree model object.

The views behave exactly in the same way as computed values: they react to any change of state. Thus we should be already familiar with this concept.

Let's try now to recap how a MobX state tree model is composed, considering we have explored the key parts:

- **Models** require an object where we describe the model state (similar to the observables in MobX).

- **Views** require an object where we specify the computed values that are linked to the application state and they react to it.

- **Actions** are the methods used by the UI for interacting with the application state.

With this in mind we can move forward analyzing the rest of the stores.

In the SearchStore there are a couple of other important things to highlight, so let's check the implementation of the computed value inside the views object:

```
get url(){
        return getEnv(self).config.getSearchURL(getParent(self).
        searchTerm);
}
```

getEnv and *getParent* are the other two methods provided by MobX state tree. The first one is used for getting access to the objects injected inside the main tree, in our case the configuration util object used for creating the final URL to use when we consume the Flickr APIs.

getParent, instead, allows us to retrieve the parent node of the tree, in our case the root that we composed with the main GalleryModel; searchTerm is an observable described inside the main model.

As we can see, this approach could result in difficult maintenance, particularly when the tree has many nested nodes. That's why we need to think twice when we work in this way: the secret here is keeping the trees with not many nested levels and to work more encapsulating the components of our application.

The functionalities in the search store are exactly the same as the previous example but expressed in the MobX state tree way.

Moving forward we can briefly take a look at the other two stores; the PhotoGalleryStore is implemented like this:

```
import { types, getParent } from 'mobx-state-tree'

const photoGalleryStore = types.model("Gallery", {
}).views(self => ({
    get totalPics(){
        return getParent(self).picsList.length;
    }
})).actions(self =>({
    setPictures(arr){
        getParent(self).setPicsList(arr);
    }
}))

export default photoGalleryStore;
```

Once again, we are communicating with the GalleryModel via the getParent method, considering the main model is composed inside the root of our state tree.

For the SelectedPictureStore, instead, the implementation is this one:

```
import { types, getParent } from "mobx-state-tree";

const selectedPictureStore = types.model({
}).actions(self => ({
    setPictureURL(url){
        getParent(self).setSelectedPictureURL(url);
    }
}))

export default selectedPictureStore;
```

And also in this case we are just setting the final URL to display and automatically the components will react to the change happening to the selectedPictureURL observable in the main model.

Overall, the porting from a MobX project to a state tree one doesn't request much effort but provides a lot of value due to its opinionated nature of doing things and enforcing rules for a better application structure.

Wrap-Up

In this chapter, we have evaluated how MobX can be used in the real world as a reactive state management providing automated and optimized derivations for improving our application performances and providing predictability.

We discovered that MobX can be used in conjunction with React, but there are also several implementations for other virtual DOM libraries like Vue.js or Snabbdom.

Last but not least we have evaluated two examples: one with MobX only; and another one with MobX state tree, an opinionated library, which provides a tree structure to our application state, mirroring the concepts behind a DOM tree and providing several utilities for composing and decorating our application state.

Architecturally speaking, MobX provides a level of flexibility that is hard to find with other frameworks, and it's the perfect companion for moving existing applications to a reactive paradigm improving their predictability and for anyone that wants to embrace the reactive paradigm quickly.

Using a MobX state tree for new applications or proof of concepts provides a quick and well-designed structure improving our productivity without compromising on quality.

And the last important point is that in both examples, we extracted the application state from the stores guaranteeing a better separation of concerns and less coupling between stores that are unaware of the existence of others maintaining their bounded context appropriately.

CHAPTER 6

SAM: A Functional Reactive Pattern

Because, you know, resilience – if you think of it in terms of the Gold Rush, then you'd be pretty depressed right now because the last nugget of gold would be gone. But the good thing is, with innovation, there isn't a last nugget.

Every new thing creates two new questions and two new opportunities.

—Jeff Bezos

In this chapter we are going to explore the SAM Pattern, less used inside the community but still part of the functional/reactive family.

SAM stands for **State-Action-Model**, three actors that we have already encountered in other frameworks, but with the SAM pattern we are going to discover a different use for them.

Let's start with saying that SAM is following the unidirectional flow pattern, also is heavily based on functional concepts; in fact functions are first-class citizens for the correct implementation of the final architecture.

Because SAM is a pattern, it's totally framework agnostic, and it can be used with MobX, Cycle.js, Angular, or any other framework we are using in a specific project, also in our Vanilla JavaScript projects if we want.

During this chapter, we explore a "vanilla" implementation of SAM in order to understand how this pattern uses the reactive paradigm for managing the data flow between objects.

© Luca Mezzalira 2018
L. Mezzalira, *Front-End Reactive Architectures*, https://doi.org/10.1007/978-1-4842-3180-7_6

Introduction to SAM

SAM was created with clear goals in mind, and we could summarize them in this way:

- **Composition**: in SAM we work a lot with composition and pure functions; this allows us to reduce the coupling between objects and easily testing in isolation different parts of the pattern.

- **Unidirectional data flow**: as we have seen for Cycle.js, also SAM is leveraging the concept of unidirectional data flow trough high-order function creating a reactive loop between the different parts of our applications.

- **Framework agnostic**: SAM is framework agnostic and therefore can be used not only on the client but also on the server if needed.

- **Passive view**: working with SAM allows us to have passive views, and they are totally decoupled from the behaviors allowing us to test a specific view in isolation and potentially change them at runtime or transpile time, maintaining the same behavior.

- **Fractal architecture**: we have already encountered in our journey Cycle.js that embraces the fractal architecture paradigm. SAM is doing the same: providing the flexibility to work with well-encapsulated components that can be put together following the same architecture principles.

Figure 6-1 provides a schematic to understand this pattern.

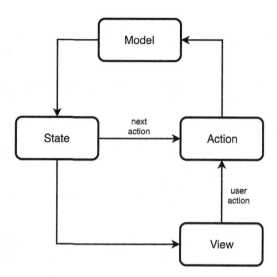

Figure 6-1. *SAM pattern schematic*

As mentioned before, SAM is composed by the state, action, and model, and the flow for a SAM project is the following one:

- An action is triggered by a user interaction, and the main responsibility is translating the user intent to data to be validated inside the model.

- The model needs to evaluate the data received by the action and it can either accept them or not.

   In case the data are not as expected, the model can decide to trigger an error or fail silently.

   The model is also responsible for maintaining the application state and triggering the state representation.

   The best way to implement a model in this pattern is using a single state tree.

- The state, unlike the name suggests, is a function that computes the state representation from the model and notifies the view that something new needs to be rendered.

   Also the state is responsible for calling the next-action-predicate, and this function called nap will invoke any automatic action that needs to be called.

The reactivity in this pattern is composed by the loop of the main actors, which are changing the state representation after every action invoked.

SAM pattern could be summarized with a mathematical formula:

View = State(viewmodel(Model.present(Action(data))), nextAction Predicate(Model))

SAM takes inspiration from React components implementation where React introduced a strong decoupling between the data to represent and the view itself; therefore any virtual DOM library fits very well in the SAM pattern.

In fact, the state representation is just providing an output that will be computed by a virtual DOM library like React, Vue.js, or Snabbdom.

Obviously, we can also think to use template libraries but the Virtual DOM ones fit better for the pattern purposes.

The state representation is not meant to keep the state but to merge the data with the virtual dom or template, retrieving the state from the model and combining it with a specific interface.

The model, as mentioned above, has to evaluate values provided by an action; it exposes only the `present` function, and it can decide to accept or refuse the data received, triggering an error or silently stopping the loop for a specific scenario.

The actions are very similar to what an intent is doing in Cycle.js: they are preparing the data to be proposed to the model. The actions can be invoked by user interactions on the UI or via the `nap` method, and this method is called after the state representation for automatically changing the model and triggering another render of the view.

SAM Pattern Data Flow

If we were to summarize with code the SAM pattern data flow, we could do it with a skeleton like this:

```
const model = {
    status: STATUS.INIT,
    present: data => {
        if(model.status === STATUS.INIT){
            model.status = STATUS.STATE1;
        }
```

```javascript
        if(Array.isArray(data)){
            model.status = STATUS.INIT;
        }

        state.render(model)
    }
};

const actions = {
    state1: (value, present) => {
        present({data: value});
    }
}

const nap = model => {
    if (model.status === STATUS.INIT) {
        actions.state1(value, model.present);
    }
}

const view = {
    init: model => {
        return <div> This is the initial view </div>
    },
    state1: model => {
        return <div> This is the state1 view </div>
    }
}

const state = {
    init: model => (model.status === STATUS.INIT),
    state1: model => (model.status === STATUS.ANOTHER_STATUS),
    render: model => {
        stateRepresentation(model);
        nap(model);
    }
}
```

```
const stateRepresentation = model => {
    let representation = <div>something went wrong!</div>

    if(state.state1(model))
        representation = view.state1(model);

    if(state.init(model))
        representation = view.init(model);

    display(representation);
};

const display = view => {
    //append the view to the DOM
}
```

Starting from the top of our skeleton, we can immediately see the model that exposes only the present method and it is validating the data proposed by any action.

When the validation succeeds, the present method invokes the state render function.

The state object is responsible for preparing the view to display based on the application state provided by the model and to call the nap method for performing other automatic actions based on the application state.

The state representation goal is composing the view (either a template or a Virtual DOM) with the application state retrieved from the model; and once everything is computed, this function invokes the display one where we are appending the UI into the DOM.

After that, the next-action-predicate checks if in a specific status of our application it needs to invoke the next action automatically without the need for the model to have complicated logic to implement.

For starting our application we can either call an action, for instance, consuming a remote endpoint; or display a static view where the user will be able to interact (searching in an input field, interacting with a button and so on).

Let's see how we can implement a simple project with SAM and React.js in order to shed some light on this reactive pattern.

A Basic Implementation of SAM

This time we want to build an interface similar to Figure 6-2.

Figure 6-2. *Our new interface*

This interface has some peculiarities, so the first thing to do would be to load the countries data provided by an open API. Then we will need to generate the list on the left of the map above where every time a user is clicking on a country name, we want to display few information on the right side of our UI, like the country name, the flag, the population size, the capital, and an interactive map showing the country coordinates.

Considering we start the application without any user interaction we are going immediately to set a default country, so we can fill up the space and provide some information on how to use our application to the final user.

In this case the next-action-predicate will help us to achieve this task.

We are going now to create the application based on the skeleton we have explored before; remember that the SAM pattern embraces the simplicity of a clean and robust architecture with the power of two programming paradigms like functional and reactive ones.

Reviewing the Example

Let's start to analyze our example from the beginning. The first thing to do is to wait until the first action for consuming a remote endpoint, retrieving the specific data requested for displaying the selected country details:

```
document.addEventListener("DOMContentLoaded", function(event) {
    actions.getCountries(REGION, model.present)
});
```

We can immediately see that we are passing to the getCountries action a default country and the present method of the model that will be invoked once the promise inside the action will be fulfilled:

```
getCountries: (region, present) => {
      fetch(URL + region)
          .then(response => response.json())
          .then(data => {
              const countries = normaliseData(data);
              present(countries);
          })
    }
```

Once we receive the response and we normalize the data filtering with only what the view needs, we call the present method injected as argument, and this method is responsible for accepting or not the data prepared by the action. Therefore we can say that these actions have the responsibility of preparing data that the model consumes and uses for then rendering a new state.

Let's see what our model looks like:

```
const model = {
    status: STATUS.INIT,
    selectedCountryID: "",
    countries: [],
    present: data => {
        if(data.selectedID !== "" || model.status === STATUS.INIT){
            model.status = STATUS.SELECT_COUNTRY;
            model.selectedCountryID = data.selectedID;
        }
```

```
        if(Array.isArray(data)){
            model.status = STATUS.INIT;
            model.countries = data;
        }

        state.render(model)
    }
};
```

The model is an object with a `status` property where we store the current
application state, a few parameters used for rendering the new state like `countries`
and `selectedCountryID`, and finally the method `present` that is invoked every time by
actions only.

Inside the `present` method we can see the checks for each single possible value we
are going to receive from an action. This could become a long list of checks, so in large
applications we would need to wrap these statements in external files for making the
code more readable and easy to manage.

Once the checks are passed the `present` function invokes the `render` method of the
state object:

```
const state = {
    init: model => (model.status === STATUS.INIT && model.countries.length
    > 0 && model.selectedCountryID == ""),
    selectCountry: model => (model.status === STATUS.SELECT_COUNTRY &&
    model.selectedCountryID !== ""),
    render: model => {
        stateRepresentation(model);
        nap(model);
    }
}
```

In the `state` object, we have some methods used for understanding in which state
the application is, like the `init` and `selectCountry` methods, and also the render
method that is split in preparing the state representation and invoking the `nap` function.

The state representation uses the application state for merging the data stored in the model with the UI to display:

```
const stateRepresentation = model => {
    let representation = <div>something went wrong!</div>

    if(state.selectCountry(model))
        representation = view.selectCountry(model);

    if(state.init(model))
        representation = view.init(model);

    display(representation);
};
```

In the snippet above we can see that every time the function is called, we are performing some checks on different application states and when we identify in which one we are, we can retrieve the correct view to pass to the display method.

This is what our view object looks like:

```
const view = {
    init: model => {
        return <div>
            <CountriesList data={model.countries}/>
            <SelectedCountry/>
        </div>
    },
    selectCountry: model => {
        const index = model.countries.findIndex( contry => contry.id ===
        model.selectedCountryID);
        const country = model.countries[index];
        return <div>
                    <CountriesList data={model.countries} action={actions.
                    selectCountry} present={model.present}/>
                    <SelectedCountry country={country}/>
                </div>
    }
}
```

Because we decided to use React, the UI is composed by a bunch of custom components where we inject some properties retrieved from the model like the countries for rendering the list of countries but also the actions and the present method. So when a user clicks on a country name we invoke the action passing the selected country unique identifier and the model's present method injected when we defined the component.

Let's have a look at the completed example:

```
import React from "react";
import ReactDOM from "react-dom";
import SelectedCountry from "./components/SelectedCountry";
import CountriesList from "./components/CountriesList";
import {STATUS, URL, REGION, INIT_COUNTRY} from "./configurations/Config";

const model = {
    status: STATUS.INIT,
    selectedCountryID: "",
    countries: [],
    present: data => {
        if(data.selectedID !== "" || model.status === STATUS.INIT){
            model.status = STATUS.SELECT_COUNTRY;
            model.selectedCountryID = data.selectedID;
        }

        if(Array.isArray(data)){
            model.status = STATUS.INIT;
            model.countries = data;
        }

        state.render(model)
    }
};

const normaliseData = data => {
    return data.map(country => {
        return {
            id: country.alpha2Code,
            name: country.name,
```

```
                lat: country.latlng[0],
                lng: country.latlng[1],
                flag: country.flag,
                capital: country.capital,
                population: country.population
            }
        })
}

const actions = {
    selectCountry: (id, present) => {
        present({selectedID: id});
    },
    getCountries: (region, present) => {
        fetch(URL + region)
            .then(response => response.json())
            .then(data => {
                const countries = normaliseData(data);
                present(countries);
            })
    }
}

const nap = model => {
    if (model.status === STATUS.INIT) {
        actions.selectCountry(INIT_COUNTRY, model.present);
    }
}

const view = {
    init: model => {
        return <div>
            <CountriesList data={model.countries}/>
            <SelectedCountry/>
        </div>
    },
```

```
    selectCountry: model => {
        const index = model.countries.findIndex( contry => contry.id ===
        model.selectedCountryID);
        const country = model.countries[index];
        return <div>
                    <CountriesList data={model.countries} action={actions.
                    selectCountry} present={model.present}/>
                    <SelectedCountry country={country}/>
                </div>
    }
}

const state = {
    init: model => (model.status === STATUS.INIT && model.countries.length
    > 0 && model.selectedCountryID == ""),
    selectCountry: model => (model.status === STATUS.SELECT_COUNTRY &&
    model.selectedCountryID !== ""),
    render: model => {
        stateRepresentation(model);
        nap(model);
    }
}

const stateRepresentation = model => {
    let representation = <div>something went wrong!</div>

    if(state.selectCountry(model))
        representation = view.selectCountry(model);

    if(state.init(model))
        representation = view.init(model);

    display(representation);
};

const display = view => {
    const app = document.getElementById("app");
    ReactDOM.render(view, app);
}
```

```
document.addEventListener("DOMContentLoaded", function(event) {
    actions.getCountries(REGION, model.present)
});
```

If we want to summarize the flow of this SAM application, we could come up with this list:

- Once the user interacts with an element inside the countries list, it triggers an action that provides the country ID to the `present` method of the model.

- The model checks which kind of data is received from the action and stores in the `selectedCountryID` the ID provided by the action.

- The model then triggers the state representation where we are assembling the new view based on the model data.

- The view is pushed to the `display` method that will append the new view state to the DOM.

- At the end we are invoking the `nap` function that checks if in the specific application state we need to trigger any automatic action or not.

SAM is an interesting pattern because it combines S.O.L.I.D. principles with different programming paradigms. When we want to implement it in a real project we need to be aware of the freedom provided by this pattern, considering at the moment there aren't many frameworks that are enforcing SAM rules.

At the same time, SAM provides us a great structure, a strong encapsulation, and applies the single responsibility principle very well for each main part of the pattern.

This allows us to test quickly and in total isolation our projects, and considering it's heavily based on pure functions, we are not going to have any side effects from them. Therefore the outcome predictability of this pattern is very high.

As I said at the beginning of the chapter, we can implement SAM in our existing architectures or we could use an architecture that bases its foundations into SAM providing a solid structure for handling elegantly the data flow of our applications.

Wrap-Up

In this chapter, we looked at another approach to reactive architectures. As we have learned, there are many interpretations and all of them are providing pros and cons to take in consideration.

SAM in particular has solid foundations with great principles to be inspired by, and the simplicity of its implementation grants us the ability to apply the SAM pattern in any project, existing or greenfield, without the need to use specific frameworks for using it.

Now it's time to look at the future of reactive paradigm and in particular how we will envision this paradigm in the front-end panorama for the next years. But this time I won't be alone, so let us move on to the last chapter of this book.

CHAPTER 7

A Reactive Future

The future belongs to those who prepare for it today.

—Malcom X

Is this the end of our journey of Reactive architectures? I have to say that's not the end at all, and probably it's just the beginning!

In this book I tried to collect some information to be really productive with Reactive Programming. Often you can find resources that explain how to use Reactive Programming with Rx.JS, for instance, but none of them clearly present concrete examples on how to implement Reactive Architectures in practice.

Reactive Architectures as well as Reactive Programming are just at the beginning of their life cycle, and there are plenty of other things to discover: viewing Reactive concepts from different angles and probably learning from the mistakes made at the beginning of this journey.

Embracing Reactive architectures right now could provide you a competitive advantage for the future of your projects and/or career.

I personally think Reactive Programming is going to impact the way we are thinking about software programming, and this paradigm has a learning curve that is far from being the easiest one, but once we understand a few key concepts, every line of code we write will become better and better.

Another important value provided by Reactive Programming is the fact we can "mix and match" with existing architectures, enhancing our projects and moving them to the next step forward, enhancing objects encapsulation and the single responsibility principles.

I don't want to spend an entire chapter talking about how I embraced the Reactive paradigm because I think it's clear that I really get into it; however I thought it would be beneficial hearing also some stories from the most active developers in the Reactive

© Luca Mezzalira 2018
L. Mezzalira, *Front-End Reactive Architectures*, https://doi.org/10.1007/978-1-4842-3180-7_7

ecosystem. Therefore, I decided to interview them and share how they envision the future of this paradigm on front-end development.

Following, you will be able to read the answers to a questionnaire I prepared for the following:

- Ben Lesh – Rx.JS 5 creator

- Michel Weststrate – MobX creator

I hope you will enjoy what these gurus have to say on the topic and that you have enjoyed this journey of Reactive Front-End Architectures.

Ben Lesh

Can you give us a brief introduction of yourself?

My name is Ben Lesh, and I'm an engineer at Google, formerly at Netflix, and I'm the development lead for RxJS.

What are you doing for the reactive community?

I'm working on making RxJS smaller, faster, and more ergonomic.

Why should a company or a developer embrace Reactive Programming?

Reactive programming enables a lot of agility in code by being able to quickly, declaratively define almost any behavior with very little code.

In your opinion, what are the Pros and the Cons of Reactive Programming?

The biggest pro is that you have a single type that can represent pretty much anything. Values that are either synchronous or asynchronous. A single value, many values, or no values at all. And because this type represents a set, there are a great number of transformations, joins, and queries you can perform on them.

The biggest con is that in order to do all of the above, you have to learn a vernacular that is particular to reactive programming. This means learning terms like mergeMap or switchMap, etc.

Which is the most important benefit provided by Reactive Programming?

The biggest benefit of reactive programming is being able to break applications down into smaller pieces of work that are truly independent from one another.

Talking about Reactive architectures, do you think there will be an evolution from where we are now? If so, which one?

I think we're about to see a lot of reactive languages start popping up. I know of two off the top of my head right now. One is a server-side reactive programming language that Facebook is working on. Another is a client-side reactive programming language being worked on by a colleague of mine.

Which framework or architecture do you usually use for your Reactive projects and why?

Over the last three years I have used Ember, React, and Angular. Angular has first-class handling for rxjs observables. Since I work on an end of the project at Google, I use Angular, but I have no favorite. However the Angular Team itself is one of my favorite groups of people so I guess I give them a little favoritism.

What is missing in the Reactive panorama?

We need more tooling for debugging in the browser. You can only do so much within a library, and it would be nice to have better tools built into Chrome to divide some of the more hairy scenarios in rxjs.

What would you change in the Reactive ecosystem?

I wish we had more contributors. I particularly wish we had a more diverse set of contributors. When I say contributors I mean pretty much anything from engineering talent to community organization. The reactive programming Community is very small even though RxJS is widely used.

Which is the best approach to start working with Reactive Programming?

I think it's best just to pull it into something like jsbin and start using it and playing with it. Try a few operators and start with things like filter, map, and scan, then move on to something like mergeMap.

Talking about the library you created, can you share with us your vision for its future?

Well in the not-too-distant future we're going to be moving away from prototype patching and using more functional-based operators. So basically we're going to have higher-order functions that return a function you can use in the let operator. There will also be more utility around that. This will allow better tree shaking, which means smaller bundles for people using rxjs with something like webpack.

I'm also working very hard on reducing the size of the library.

If you could change one thing right now in your library, what would it be?

I'm already working on it. Mostly I just wish it was less work so I could be done already. Haha.

Can you share one trick of your library that few developers understand or are using in this moment?

I think I talked about this in my talk at AngularConnect last year. But it's important for people to realize what they're doing is setting up a chain of Observers. And that observers all have the guarantee that if error or complete is called on them they can no longer next. So if you want to handle an error and keep an observable alive, you need to isolate that Observer chain in a merge map and punctuated with a catch or a retry.

Reactive programming in 10 years, what is your prevision?

I predict that it'll be a little bit more mainstream than it is now. It's one of those infectious ideas that's hard to convey to people but once they get it they can't help but tell other people.

Anything else to add?

I'd really like to thank Eric Meijer, Matt Podwysocki for creating RxJS, and the rest of the Rx community for supporting RxJS these last few years.

Michel Weststrate

Can you give us a brief introduction of yourself?

I have been programming for almost 20 years, and 10 years professionally. Started with Pascal, Object Pascal as a kid, then went to C# and Java and finally ended up doing mainly JavaScript / TypeScript. The pace of innovation in the JavaScript and TypeScript world makes it a very interesting environment.

What are you doing for the reactive community?

Over a year ago I open sourced the MobX reactive programming library. It was initially developed for Mendix, but it solves many of the problems present in the React community (although it is generically applicable and used without the React community as well).

Why should a company or a developer embrace Reactive Programming?

If reactive programming is well applied, it increases decoupling and increases the declarativity of the code. This is the result of the fact that Reactive Programming separates the description of behavior from the enforcement of that behavior; with Reactive Programming, behavior of a value is declared once, while the consistent execution of that behavior is enforced by the Reactive Programming library. I often compare it with civil laws versus laws of nature. The former state a wish, but they need law enforcement to ensure the behavior is applied in the majority of the cases. Laws of nature, on the other hand, cannot be violated intentionally or accidentally. The system simply guarantees consistency.

As an example, MobX guarantees that any React component that renders a piece of data will update as soon as that data is changed. It doesn't matter how the component got the data. It will update. Like towing a skateboard with a cart; if the car starts moving, so will the skateboard. Simply because you introduced a rope tying the two things together. You don't bother enforcing that relation. The relation is no longer the idea of a relation, it is an actual one. And nature, or MobX, will always do its job.

In your opinion, what are the Pros and the Cons of Reactive Programming?

Pro: More declarative in nature. You just specify what should happen. Then it is up to the system to figure out when it should happen.

Pro: Inversion of control: You don't care about who is listening to the event you are emitting, or the value you are changing. This increases decoupling significantly. Eases refactoring, etc.

Pro: Better scalable architecture: Because producer and consumer are strictly separated, you are more flexible in changing either of them. It avoids the spaghetti code related to all the effects that need to happen when updating a value, which is so typical for large imperative projects.

Con: Inversion of control also means an additional level of indirection. So when doing using Reactive Programming, between the event emitted or the value changed, there is always some library internals you have to debug through, before you arrive at the effect they cause. (Some libraries will even run the effects on a different stack, making this significantly harder.)

Con: Reactive Programming code is often harder to grasp. Especially when using observable streams, you need to know the meaning of a whole range of stream-specific operators before you are able to read what was intended.

Which is the most important benefit provided by Reactive Programming?

Decoupling, then declarativity.

Talking about Reactive architectures, do you think there will be an evolution from where we are now? If so, which one?

I think reactivity across system boundaries is an area that will evolve significantly in the future. Meteor did some groundbreaking work here in the past, and we see this idea still in horizonDB, firebase, and GraphQL subscriptions. I think that in the future we will consume and react to events in the database just as easily as we react to events in the client-side state.

Another dream I have is to introduce a reactive (virtual?) filesystem and build our build tools on top of that. If each file is just a reactive stream of data, we will able to combine the efficiency of Makefiles with real-time updates we have started to appreciate so much in file watchers. With proper dependency analysis, we will remove all the quirks where a chained watcher will build too much, too early, or in the wrong order.

Which framework or architecture do you usually use for your Reactive projects and why?

There are two mainstream categories of reactivity: Reactive streams and Reactive values (or cells). Reactive streams are very powerful if the derivation of a value requires knowledge of the past or time. Examples of this are debouncing events, network requests etc., producing values from a sliding window of past values etc. In these cases the Rx* family provides very powerful tools.

However, when deriving values, it only requires knowledge of the present, reactive data cells are much more convenient to work with. This is the mechanism that made spreadsheets so popular. With reactive data cells, one does often not need to set up explicit subscriptions, and one can use all the first-class operators of the language, rather than having stream-specific libraries. This mechanism makes libraries like Knockout, Meteor, Vuejs, and MobX so approachable.

What is missing in the Reactive panorama?

Reactive file system interactions.

What would you change in the Reactive ecosystem?

There are two important mainstream categories of reactive systems: Reactive streams, and (transparent) reactive cells (or values). They both solve quite different problems, but failing to recognize the distinction leads to quite some confusion.

Which is the best approach to start working with Reactive Programming?

Build a web application with React and MobX to manage the client-side state. Then add RxJS to debounce search queries and network requests.

Talking about the library you created, can you share with us your vision for its future?

MobX is barely visible in your code; it is mostly there at the background. I want to make it even more invisible when Proxies are standardized in browsers.

If you could change one thing right now in your library, what would it be?

Separate the reactivity algorithms and core api from the observable data collections. That would make it easier to target different environments (e.g., ES3 or Proxy-supporting environments) and make MobX more accessible for those who don't like the property wrapping it like it does on objects.

Can you share one trick of your library that few developers understand or are using in this moment?

Keep side effects really small. But derive as much data as possible. It's often surprising how much one can derive from the state. It keeps imperative code to a minimum.

Reactive programming in 10 years, what is your prevision?

More closely connected front-end / back-end architectures where the notion of client-side state largely disappears for domain data.

Anything else to add?

Can you send me a copy of the book :)

Index

A

Angular
App.component.ts, 44
architecture view, 42
CalculatorModel.ts, 48
calculator project, 43
command pattern, 47
concepts, 42
meaning, 41
NgModule, 42
properties, 44
template system, 44
UpdateTotalService.ts, 47
Architectures
definition, 19
design decisions, 19–20
front-end ecosystem, 20
JavaScript (*see* JavaScript)
MV* architectures (*see* MV* architectures)
timeline, 20

B

Backpressure, 90
component code, 94
componentDidMount method, 95
final output, 91
generateProducer method, 93
loss-less strategy, 91

lossy strategy, 91
main application, 92
React component, 92
sampleTime operator, 94
stock value, 92
zip operator, 91

C

Cold observable
definition, 77
output, 78–79
re-instantiates, 80
with Rx.JS, 78
startWith operator, 79
Command pattern, 47
Communicating Sequential
Processes (CSP), 12
Cycle.js
circular dependency, 101, 109
communication via streams, 109
computer's *vs.* user's input sense, 98
DOM driver, 100–101, 103, 106
flat stream (flatten method), 106
getRequest function, 105
HTTP driver, 105
implementation, 106
interaction, 97
key concepts, 100
libraries, 100

183

© Luca Mezzalira 2018
L. Mezzalira, *Front-End Reactive Architectures*, https://doi.org/10.1007/978-1-4842-3180-7

Get the eBook for only $5!

Why limit yourself?

With most of our titles available in both PDF and ePUB format, you can access your content wherever and however you wish—on your PC, phone, tablet, or reader.

Since you've purchased this print book, we are happy to offer you the eBook for just $5.

To learn more, go to http://www.apress.com/companion or contact support@apress.com.

Apress®

Printed in the United States
By Bookmasters